Learning thro

Movement in the

Early Years

EARLY
YEARS

You might also like the following early years books from Critical Publishing

The Critical Years: Early Years Development from Conception to 5
Tim Gully
978-1-909330-73-3 In print

Developing as a Reflective Early Years Professional: A Thematic Approach
Hayes, Daly, Duncan, Gill and Whitehouse
978-1-909682-21-4 In print

Early Years Placements: A Critical Guide to Outstanding Work-based Learning
Jackie Musgrave and Nicola Stobbs
978-1-909682-65-8 In print

Early Years Policy and Practice: A Critical Alliance
Pat Tomlinson
978-1-909330-61-0 In print

Global Childhoods
Monica Edwards
978-1-909682-69-6 In print

International Perspectives on Early Years Workforce Development
Ed Verity Campbell-Barr and Jan Georgeson
978-1-909682-77-1 In print

Well-being in the Early Years
Bligh, Chambers, Davison, Lloyd, Musgrave, O'Sullivan and Waltham
978-1-909330-65-8 In print

Most of our titles are also available in a range of electronic formats. To order please go to our website www.criticalpublishing.com or contact our distributor, NBN International, 10 Thornbury Road, Plymouth PL6 7PP, telephone 01752 202301 or email orders@nbninternational.com.

Learning through Movement in the Early Years

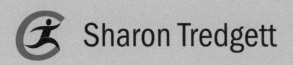 Sharon Tredgett

EARLY YEARS

First published in 2015 by Critical Publishing Ltd

British Library Cataloguing in Publication Data
A CIP record for this book is available from the British Library

ISBN: 978-1-909682-81-8

This book is also available in the following e-book formats:

MOBI ISBN: 978-1-909682-82-5
EPUB ISBN: 978-1-909682-83-2
Adobe e-book ISBN: 978-1-909682-84-9

Cover and text design by Greensplash Limited
Project Management by Out of House Publishing
Printed and bound in Great Britain by Bell & Bain, Glasgow

Critical Publishing
152 Chester Road
Northwich
CW8 4AL
www.criticalpublishing.com

Contents

Author's note

This book focuses on one aspect of learning: the importance of movement in the early years. While the text details development up to the age of 8, there is full acknowledgement that the brain continues to develop beyond then. When reading the book, it is vital that you remain mindful of and make connections with other aspects of learning. The text also fully acknowledges the need for parental and multi-agency partnerships in supporting the child's development.

Case studies

All cases studies are authentic and represent a cross-section of early years settings.

Definitions

Definitions for crawling and creeping vary depending on which book you read and authors' preferences. For the purpose of this book the following definitions have been used:

- crawling – when a child moves themselves along the floor on their tummy;
- creeping – when a child is moving on their hands and knees with their tummy away from the floor.

Sharon Tredgett, 2015

Meet the author

Sharon Tredgett is an early years practitioner with over 25 years' experience. She spent her early career working within children's centres and for Sure Start before becoming a trainer and consultant specifically around children's learning through movement. She currently works for Leeds City Council as part of the learning improvement team and has devised, written and delivered a range of training programmes to a wide spectrum of early years practitioners both within and outside of the local authority. She has written accredited units on learning through movement and continues to assess and moderate on these. Sharon continues to build her reputation as a trainer and consultant within her area of expertise.

Acknowledgements

Heartfelt thanks go to the family, friends and colleagues who have journeyed with, believed in and invested in me over the years and throughout the writing of this book. Your support, encouragement and insights have been invaluable.

For many years my journey has been inspired and informed by precious children, their families and the practitioners that work with them. I am grateful to all who have been willing to share their stories, without which this book would not have been possible.

In addition to those who wish to remain anonymous I would like to thank the following individuals for specific contributions to this book:

Case studies

Kate Johnson, day care manager, Parklands Children's Centre, Leeds

Samantha Thompson and Emma Baxter, Broadgate Primary School

Christine and Mike, Sunshine Childminders

Catherine Oldfield, early years professional, Tadpoles Day Nursery

Catherine Sullivan, early years practitioner

Sarah Parkinson, assistant headteacher in 2014, Alwoodley Primary School

The drawing of the brain, Chapter 1, page 2

Laura France Hodgkinson

Written piece on emotional development, Chapter 3, page 45

Penny Vine, trainer with the Centre for Nonviolent Communication.

1 Early movement and the brain

Key messages

- Movement opportunities in the early years are crucial since they impact on the development of the brain, laying the foundation for learning.

- Movement is essential for a child's motor and sensory development.

- It is important that you have a good understanding of what sensory integration is and are able to support this development by providing a rich and stimulating enabling environment.

- Movement is vital for reflex integration. 'Reflex integration takes place as a result of a combination of the maturation in the central nervous system and physical interaction with the environment' (Goddard Blythe, 2008, p 141).

- Partnership with parents is crucial for a child's learning and development. 'The EYFS seeks to provide partnership working between practitioners and with parents and/or carers' (Department for Education, 2012, p 2).

Introduction

Chapter 1 gives an educational perspective on the importance of early movement opportunities and is not meant to be used for diagnosing children. Whilst focusing on the importance of movement as a crucial way children learn, it also seeks to highlight characteristics which offer a wider perspective and insight into areas that can often be referred to as behavioural issues.

Movement and the brain

At birth the brain contains about 100 billion specialised brain cells called neurons (Dommett, 2012). These neurons send electronic signals to develop connections with each other, forming circuits. Whilst some of these are already intricately connected at birth, ongoing experiences enable the links between the neurons to continue to be strengthened and others to be formed (Featherstone, 2008). Strong circuits are formed around the brain, including those of motor skills and behaviour, and all circuits are interconnected. The nervous system must go through a developmental process for the brain to grow and function well. Supported through motor and sensory opportunities, this process is referred to as neurological organisation. 'We must respect the slow, but magnificent growth process of the central nervous system in the first six to eight years of life' (Lamont, n.d.).

As a practitioner, you need to provide a positive and permissive learning environment where new experiences and repetition can take place. A lack of these experiences will see a weakening of the connections. Where connections are no longer used or needed they go through a natural process called pruning (Stiles, 2012).

The organisation and structure of the brain

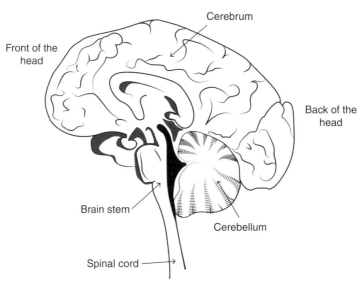

Figure 1.1 *The human brain.*

Together, the brain and the spinal cord form our central nervous system. The spinal cord takes messages from the brain to the body and from the body to the brain. The brain is often described as having three main parts: the cerebrum; the cerebellum; and the brain stem.

*   The cerebrum is the largest part of the brain and it enables intellectual functioning such as thought, memory, language, and awareness to take place. It is made up of four lobes: frontal, parietal, occipital and temporal.

    –   The frontal lobe supports aspects including reasoning, problem solving, planning, speech and movement.

    –   The parietal lobe supports aspects including perception and orientation.

- – The occipital lobe is supportive of visual processing.

- – The temporal lobe is supportive of auditory perception, memory and speech.

- Cerebellum means 'little brain' in Latin. Containing more neurons than any other part of the brain (Hannaford, 2005), it is crucial for motor development as it enables the integration and coordination of movement including posture, timing and precision. The cerebellum receives sensory input from the body and from the higher centres of the brain.

- The brain stem is made up of three main parts, the medulla, the pons (which means 'bridge') and the mid brain (Samuel, n.d.).

  - – The medulla maintains the essential body functions of breathing and heart rate.

  - – The pons is involved in motor control and sensory processing.

  - – The mid brain, whilst smaller in size than the medulla and pons, supports vision and hearing (Restak, 1984) and eye and body movement.

Sensory integration

Sensory integration refers to the processing and integration of messages from the senses in the body and environment, such as temperature, pain and light, by the brain. This has a daily impact on learning and behaviour. 'Until a child reaches about the age of 7, the brain is primarily a sensory processing machine' (Ayres, 2005, p 7), with the child's brain getting meaning through sensations, mainly through movement. The ability to integrate sensory information is crucial as it enables a child to move, learn and behave appropriately.

Sensory systems begin to develop in the womb (Stock Kranowitz, 2005). As they become integrated, a child develops a well-balanced and organised system giving them the capacity to engage in learning. Children naturally seek the sensations they need to help organise and feed their brains. 'The sensory integration that occurs in moving, talking and playing is the groundwork for the more complex sensory integration that is necessary for reading, writing and good behaviour' (Ayres, 2005, p 8). Movements that take place in the early years such as reaching, grasping, tummy time, crawling, creeping, climbing, spinning and swinging all support sensory integration.

Proprioception, the vestibular system and tactile senses are the three basic sensory systems that enable children to function well and that impact on learning and behaviour, yet they are not always recognised within the early years. Proprioception and the vestibular systems are intrinsic, with proprioception enabling the body to know where it is in space and the vestibular system maintaining balance.

Most early years practitioners know that the five external senses are sight, hearing, taste, touch and smell. Equally, they are confident in offering rich opportunities to develop these senses within the learning environment. However, there is not always the same level of consistency and confidence in understanding the three basic sensory systems that enable children to function well.

The level of sensory integration in children varies from high to low. Taking each of the three sensory systems in turn, this section offers definitions and gives lists of examples where a child may not have a well-integrated sensory system with the brain. Those children with a low level may have an over- or under-responsive system or actively seek out sensory sensations.

The lists are not comprehensive, nor do they imply that children will display all of the characteristics or have a sensory processing disorder or sensory integration dysfunction (difficulties in integrating sensory information). The intention here is to offer you an insight into and give perspective on aspects that relate to, and have an impact on, learning and behaviour. They are taken and modified from the work of the authors named at the end of each list.

Proprioception sense

Definition: proprioception comes from the Latin word *proprius*, meaning 'one's own'.

Proprioception is the sense of 'position', which begins to develop in the womb. From around 4 months, the foetus begins to make more intricate movements, thus developing an awareness of the space around them (Tallack, 2006). It is this sense that enables the body to know where it is in relation to space and where body parts are in relation to each other. It provides the child with a confidence in moving around their environment with good motor control. Muscles and joints have proprioception receptors telling the brain which joints are moving, enabling the body to respond to the stretching of muscles (Kranowitz, 2003). Along with the position of the body they also tell the brain how quickly the body is moving and how much pressure is being applied. Proprioception is constantly aligning all of the body. Much proprioception functions at an unconscious level. It is therefore not unusual when children are having 'growth spurts' for them to demonstrate a lower level of coordination skills.

Children who do not yet have a well-integrated proprioception sense may:

- be uncertain/anxious when moving around in a space;
- try to avoid and lack confidence in physical activities/PE;
- have poor body posture, leaning forwards or resting their head on their arm whilst sitting at the table;
- bump into objects and people, knock things over or trip up more easily;
- hold their pencil too tightly, breaking the point, or equally hold it too lightly, resulting in very faint marks on the page;
- have poor motor control;
- demonstrate difficulty when walking up and down stairs;
- break items much more easily;
- need to see what they are trying to do, i.e. fasten a button;
- show an inaccurate use of strength when holding and lifting objects.

(Ayres 2005, Stock Kranowitz 2003, Stock Kranowitz 2005,
Macintyre and McVitty 2004)

CASE STUDY

Ruby and PE

Ruby was 5 years old and was in her last term of Reception. Tuesday afternoon was PE. Slowly and reluctantly, Ruby would begin getting changed. Always the last to finish changing, she would often be heard saying 'I don't like PE' as she walked to the hall. During the PE session she would appear more relaxed and engaged whilst taking part in activities near to the floor. On closer observation, Ruby could be seen to be focusing intently as she tried to fasten the buttons and zip on her clothes.

Reflective question

» *Consider the possibility that Ruby may not yet have well-developed proprioception. How, as a practitioner, would you seek to support Ruby physically and emotionally? Explain your answer.*

Vestibular sense

The vestibular system controls the sense of movement and balance. As the sense that enables the body to know where it is in relation to gravity, it is essential within daily life. It supports the orientation of the body and visual and auditory senses in space. 'The pathway linking the vestibular system to the brain stem is in place by 12 weeks (in the womb), and is the first tract in the brain to mature' (Goddard Blythe 2008, p 170). It functions at a subcortical/unconscious level in the cerebellum part of the brain. The vestibular system enables children to maintain balance whilst standing in one position, and whilst moving around and changing speed and position. Vestibular receptors are located in the inner ear: the semicircular canal identifies rotary movements and otoliths identify linear movements (Lane, 2002). In essence, the vestibular sense enables us to maintain balance, coordinate movements and vision, develop bilateral integration (using both sides of the body at the same time) and maintain an upright position. 'When the body and head move, the vestibular system is activated, and the eye muscles strengthen as they move in response' (Hannaford, 2005, p 115). Sensory information that passes through the vestibular system is then integrated with other sensory information and sent to the cerebellum.

Children who have an over-responsive vestibular system may:

- have a strong dislike of and avoid playing on swings, roundabouts and slides;
- move more slowly/hesitate and be cautious;
- ask for support from a familiar adult when engaged in physical activities;
- articulate a fear of falling when moving around;
- hold tightly on to the rail/banister when climbing up or going down stairs;
- be insecure in large and open spaces.

Children who have an under-responsive vestibular system may:

- spend endless time spinning without becoming dizzy;
- not protect themselves when they are off-balance and about to fall over;
- actively search and engage in fast movements/activities such as spinning, rocking and jumping;
- need to constantly move to engage in learning;
- love being upside-down, playing on the swings and see-saws longer than their peers;
- find it difficult to sit upright and prefer to complete activities lying down.

(Ayres 2005, Stock Kranowitz 2003, Stock Kranowitz 2005, Macintyre and McVitty 2004)

CASE STUDY

Grace

Grace was a sociable child who was popular with her peers. To walk from her Reception classroom to the dinner hall, Grace had to climb up a set of six stairs. Ever cautious, she would wait for her peers to go first before holding the rail tightly and climbing the stairs. Her return journey displayed the same characteristics. Outside in the playground, Grace would often ask to hold the hand of the practitioner.

Reflective question

» *As a practitioner, how would you support Grace and what movement opportunities would you look to provide?*

Tactile sense

The tactile system refers to the information that is sent to the brain from the touch receptors that cover the whole of the body. It registers information such as temperature, pain, light touch and deep pressure (Lane, 2002), is the largest sensory system and also the first sensory system to develop in the womb (Ayres, 2005).

Children who have an over-responsive tactile sense may:

- be reluctant to engage in creative activities and get their hands dirty;
- dislike other children in their space, and prefer to be at the front of the line;
- reject light touch;
- demonstrate a dislike of having their hair washed, teeth brushed, nails cut;
- be seen to become fidgety at group times, needing to hold something;
- choose not to be barefoot in activities on sand or grass, for example;

- walk on tiptoe;
- have a strong preference for not wearing long trousers, long-sleeved tops and clothes in contact with the skin;
- find the labels in their clothes uncomfortable against their skin;
- dislike PE;
- have a heightened response to pain.

Children who have an under-responsive tactile sense may:

- show very little response to hurting themselves or standing on something sharp;
- not respond to being squashed in a line;
- show no response to wet sleeves after playing in the water tray;
- only show a response to very firm touch;
- not be aware that they are hurting other children or hug them too tightly;
- comfortably walk on tactile surfaces that most other children find uncomfortable.

Children who display both over- or under-tactile responses may be children who:

- need to hold something at group time;
- have poor body awareness.

(Ayres 2005, Stock Kranowitz 2003, Stock Kranowitz 2005, Macintyre and McVitty 2004)

CASE STUDY

A parent's experience

Sensory disorder and its impact within the early years

I had worked with children under 5 and their families for 15 years when I gave birth to my son, Jack. As a baby he had many movement opportunities and aged 7 months he belly-crawled cross-laterally. When settling Jack, I noticed that he would settle quicker when there was a stronger rocking sensation. When he reached the tantrum phase he did so with a passion and nothing would appease him. From morning till night, tasks such as getting dressed and brushing his teeth and hair would result in a battle. Jack would refuse to wear certain items of clothing. At home he would strip off and be happy in his underpants. No matter how cold it was he didn't want to wear a coat. Gloves, hats and accessories were a definite no. Jack's behaviour and emotions ruled everything.

At nursery he would find himself in altercations with other children on a daily basis: pulling hair, pushing and biting. He was still a 'biter' at 4 years old and would run in and greet people by biting them or pushing them over.

Jack was achieving all his milestones. Whenever I talked with him about what had happened, he would tell me 'my brain told me to do it'. Over a three-year period I went to see the GP, spoke to staff at the nursery and saw three different educational psychologists.

As an early years practitioner, strategies I had confidently shared with parents for years to improve behaviour just didn't seem to be having any impact with my own son.

By the time Jack was in school I was still getting daily reports of altercations. He can't stand still in line, he's bumping into children. He's leaning on others at story time, when he's talking to others he's too close, he's hit someone. He always went into school neatly dressed and came out with holes in his trousers, shirt hanging out and dirty.

Following an appointment at the Regional Child Development Centre I was told that Jack would benefit from seeing an occupational therapist. Jack had lax ligaments that were impacting on his behaviours and emotional well-being. I came away with a leaflet about sensory disorder.

I rang the occupational therapist, who reassured me. She explained why Jack didn't like to wear clothes. It was a sensory response and he was taking in too much information through his skin. He was in a permanently stressed state and therefore the smallest change in his environment would send him 'over the edge' into a tantrum as he was constantly trying to adapt to his surroundings. For Jack, it was like having a spider crawling across his skin all the time and putting him into 'shudder' mode.

She talked about how Jack was looking for the appropriate information from his surroundings. If his senses were too strong he'd want to be quiet, suck things or be rocked to soothe him. If he needed more information he wanted things to be loud, to chew things or look for rotary activities as a stimulus. There was no consistency.

I booked a series of appointments. The equipment in the room replicated the movement sessions that I'd been involved in through work. I watched whilst Jack played games in spinners, pulling himself along on skateboards and enjoyed a swing in the net. Jack is now 15; he is still tall at 6 feet 6 inches. He is a well-rounded young man who recognises the physical sensations in his body that relate to his emotions. He knows what makes him anxious and how it impacts on him. As a parent I love him and am so proud of him.

Reflective questions

»   *Having now recognised some specific behaviours relating to sensory disorder, how would you support and ensure that Jack's individual needs were met?*

»   *Given the case study, explain how you would effectively work in partnership with the parent.*

»   *Reflecting on the case study, what are the key messages relating to sensory disorder that need to be acknowledged and approached with consistency within any early years team?*

» *Are all difficult behaviours really behavioural issues or are they indicative of children needing to support their sensory feedback system? Think about some recent examples from your setting.*

Reflexes

A reflex is an automatic response to a stimulus without conscious thought. 'Reflexes are the primary teachers of basic motor skills' (Goddard Blythe, 2008, p 142). The more a child moves, the better the control they gain over their movements. 'Movement helps to map the brain, and reflexes provide a child with some of the earliest pathways' (Goddard Blythe, 2008, pp 142–3).

Whilst in the womb, the brain is not immediately in control of movements (Maayan, 2013).

Primitive reflexes

Primitive reflexes develop when a baby is in the womb. At nine weeks after conception the first series of primitive reflexes start to take place/emerge (Goddard Blythe, 2008). The more the foetus moves, the stronger the primitive reflexes grow. Movement plays a vital role here in stimulating the growth of muscles and the strengthening of joints. Reflexes support a child's cognitive and sensory development as well as motor development.

These reflexes become integrated at between 6 and 12 months, when connections to the higher brain (cerebrum) have been developed. As the higher brain takes control, the early primitive reflexes are no longer needed. As the baby's brain and nervous system continue to develop through opportunities to engage and explore by means of significant early movement, primitive reflexes begin to become integrated. Should primitive reflexes remain heightened, there may be an impact on learning and behaviour.

It is important that you gain an understanding of primitive reflexes and fundamental that you have insight into possible indicators where children's primitive reflexes have been retained. Focusing on just some of the recognised primitive reflexes, this section offers definitions and highlights some possible indicators that they have not been integrated. They are taken and modified from the work of the authors named at the end of the list.

Rooting and sucking reflexes

The rooting reflex can be identified when the cheek near the edge of a baby's mouth is lightly touched and the head turns to that same side, with the mouth opening in preparation for sucking. As the baby pushes its tongue forward, contact is made with the nipple/teat and the baby naturally begins to suck.

Possible indicators of a retained rooting and sucking reflex:

*   ongoing dribbling;
*   speech problems;

- difficulty in swallowing and chewing;
- hypersensitivity around the lips and mouth.

Palmer and planter reflexes

Young babies demonstrate an active and strong palmer reflex when the palm of the hand is touched, causing the fingers to flex and grasp. Whilst it is not always as strong, the planter reflex functions in the same way when the sole of the foot is touched.

Possible indicators of retained palmer/planter reflexes:

- poor fine motor skills;
- an unusual pencil grip with poor thumb and finger opposition;
- difficulty in writing as a result of tactile hypersensitivity;
- walking on tiptoe.

Tonic labyrinthine reflex

Supporting the baby's early response to gravity through a change in head position, the tonic labyrinthine reflex (TLR) has a forwards and backwards movement. When the head leans forwards, the body curls up into a foetal position and as the head leans backwards, the body stretches and lengthens out. Both movements increase muscle tone and in the long term they support balance and stability in the upright position. 'It takes up to 3–3½ years for the TLR to be fully inhibited by the higher centres in the brain, indicating just how many stages and skills need to be layered one upon the other before control of balance and tonus become established' (Goddard Blythe, 2005, p 37).

Possible indictors of a retained tonic reflex:

- poor balance;
- spatial and orientation difficulties;
- issues with visual perception (judging space and depth);
- poor muscle control causing children to lean side to side and tip forwards;
- difficulty keeping the head up.

Symmetrical tonic neck reflex

The symmetrical tonic neck reflex (STNR) can often be seen when a baby is getting ready to creep. Firstly the baby's head is face down, with bent arms and legs starting to straighten. Secondly they lift their head facing forwards, extend their arms and bring their legs to a kneeling position. It is not unusual to see babies rocking backwards and forwards before they begin to creep. The reflex supports the development of body posture and near and far vision (Blomberg, 2011).

Possible indicators of a retained STNR:

- poor eye–hand coordination;

- poor muscle control and body posture causing the child to lean forward;

- choosing to sit in the 'w' position;

- difficulties with vertical tracking.

Asymmetrical tonic neck reflex

The asymmetrical tonic neck reflex (ATNR) can be identified when a baby is lying down with its head turned to one side. The arm and leg on the side it is facing extend out in the same direction, with the opposite arm and leg in a bent position. This reflex therefore affects the muscle tone differently on each side of the body depending on which side the head is turning to (Goddard Blythe, 2005). As the head moves in conjunction with the hand, connections supporting eye–hand coordination and perception are established.

Possible indicators of a retained ATNR:

- difficulties with balance and coordination;

- difficulties crossing the midline/bilateral integration;

- difficulties with visual tracking and copying from a board/screen as the eye and the hand want to move together.

Moro reflex

In the early months, babies are unable to perceive whether a situation is a threat to them. The Moro reflex triggers the fight/flight system and can be recognised, for example, when a baby is startled by a sudden noise or change in position. In response they take in a deep breath, extend their arms and legs out before drawing them back in towards their body and often crying. As this reflex becomes integrated at around 4 months, the baby begins to look for the source of what has startled them. Over time this reflex becomes the adult startle reflex.

Possible indicators of a retained Moro reflex:

- finding new situations difficult and showing emotions of being anxious/fearful;

- sudden and unanticipated changes in behaviour;

- difficulties in catching a ball or other fast-moving objects coming towards them;

- dislike of unexpected noises and changes in light;

- being easily distracted and finding it difficult to pay attention to one aspect.

(Blomberg, 2011, Goddard Blythe 2005, Goddard Blythe 2008)

CASE STUDY

Sophie

Whilst secure in her familiar classroom environment and daily routine, Sophie would become anxious when there was any change. It was also noticeable that she would become very upset if there was a loud and unexpected noise. Whilst playing and interacting with her peers, Sophie was observed to want to take the lead and direct the play.

Reflective question

Alongside finding change and filtering out noise difficult, it is important to remember that where children have a retained Moro reflex they will respond to a situation first and process afterwards, which may result in them displaying impulsive and inappropriate behaviour (Goddard Blythe, 2005).

» *How would you support these children in your setting?*

CASE STUDY

Alice

At the age of 16 months, Alice began attending her local children's centre. She had been diagnosed with severe hypotonia (low muscle tone or tension), which had implications, particularly in relation to her physical development. Partnership with the family and other professionals was essential. Whilst Alice could sit independently within a stimulating and enabling environment, she showed frustration at being unable to move around. As the centre was already working with a movement approach, and through consultation with all involved, movements and sensory activities were identified that would support Alice. Starting with lots of sensory work around the feet and progressing to lots of floor-based movement, Alice would spend time on her tummy. Three months after beginning these movement activities, Alice rolled independently from her tummy to her back. There was a noticeable increase in her independence, which saw a reduction in her frustration as she began to reach, stretch and roll. Alice's awareness of her own body developed greatly. After six months, she began to pull herself up on the furniture and walk around it whilst holding on to it. One year later, Alice took her first steps unaided, and totally amazed all the professionals working with her. She is now a confident little girl making ongoing progress. All those involved agreed that early movement opportunities played a vital role in her development.

Reflective question

» *Partnership work is crucial. Reflecting on your current practice, how could you ensure this was strengthened and further developed? Share your thoughts.*

Practical task

» *Having highlighted that proprioception, the vestibular system and tactile senses are the three basic sensory systems that enable children to function well and impact on learning and behaviour, and given that they are not always recognised within the early years, reflect on the key messages of this chapter and develop a concise presentation through which you could share their importance with colleagues. Remember, you are only looking to share an educational perspective here.*

Reflective questions

» *'Secure balance is inseparable from the development of postural control, which in turn is supported by information from the visual, proprioception and motor systems' (Goddard Blythe, 2005, p 17). Within your early years setting, what movement opportunities would you provide to support this area of development?*

» *Given that the precision of early movement is important for providing a foundation for future movement (Bly, 2011), opportunities for children to spend time on the floor engaging in these movements are crucial and yet they do not always take place. What could be the reasons for this? List and reflect on your answers.*

Summary

I've learned that people will forget what you said, people will forget what you did, but people will never forget how you made them feel.

Angelou (n.d.)

In seeking to identify the importance of motor and sensory integration in a child's early years, this chapter has also offered an educational perspective on a number of responses made by children, which can sometimes be referred to as behavioural issues. Having an increased knowledge and understanding in this area will enable you to support and respond positively and appropriately to children's individual physical and emotional needs.

Further reading

The following books will give you an increased knowledge in the area of sensory integration and primitive reflexes by specialists in this field. They offer theory and practical guidance for both parents and practitioners.

Ayres, A J (2005) *Sensory Integration and the Child: Understanding Hidden Sensory Challenges*, 25th anniversary edition. Los Angeles: Western Psychological Services.

Goddard Blythe, S (2005) *The Well Balanced Child: Movement and Early Learning*, revised edition. Stroud, Gloucestershire: Hawthorn Press.

Stock Kranowitz, C (2003) *The Out-of-Sync Child Has Fun: Activities for Kids with Sensory Processing Disorder*, revised edition. New York: Perigee.

You may also find the DVD below a useful resource:

Pioneer Productions (2005) *In the Womb: Life's Precious First Journey*. Rocket Rights/Pioneer Productions.

References

Angelou, M Brainy Quotes. Available at: www.brainyquote.com/quotes/authors/m/maya_angelou. html, accessed 4 April 2015.

Ayres, A J (2005) *Sensory Integration and the Child: Understanding Hidden Sensory Challenges*, 25th anniversary edition. Los Angeles: Western Psychological Services.

Blomberg, H (2011) *Movements That Heal: Rhythmic Movement Training and Primitive Reflex Integration*. Sunnybank Hills, QLD, Australia: BookPal.

Bly, L (2011) *Components of Typical and Atypical Motor Development*. Laguna Beach, CA: Neuro-Development Treatment Association, Inc.

Department for Education (2012) *Statutory Framework for the Early Years Foundation Stage: Setting the Standards for Learning, Development and Care for Children from Birth to Five*. Runcorn, Cheshire: Department for Education.

Dommett, E (2012) The Structure of the Human Brain, in Woodhead M and Oates, J (eds) *Early Childhood in Focus 7: Developing Brains*. Milton Keynes: Open University.

Featherstone, S (2008) Practice Makes Perfect: How the Growing Brain Makes Sense of Experiences, in Featherstone, Sand Featherstone, P, *Like Bees, Not Butterflies: Child-Initiated Learning in the Early Years*. London: A&C Black/Featherstone Education.

Goddard Blythe, S (2005) *The Well-Balanced Child: Movement and Early Learning*, revised edition. Stroud, Gloucestershire: Hawthorn Press.

Goddard Blythe, S (2008) *What Babies and Children Really Need*. Stroud, Gloucestershire: Hawthorn Press.

Hannaford, C. (2005) *Smart Moves: Why Learning Is Not All in Your Head*, 2nd edition. Salt Lake City, UT: Great River Books.

Lamont, B (n.d.) Learning and movement. [online] Available at: www.developmentalmovement.org/upload/Learning%20and%20Movement.pdf, accessed 4 April 2015.

Lane, S J (2002) Structure and Function of the Sensory Systems, in Bundy, A C, Lane, S J and Murray, E A, *Sensory Integration: Theory and Practice*, 2nd edition. Philadelphia: F A Davis Company.

Maayan, I. (2013) The Embryo Project Encyclopedia: In the womb (2005), by Toby McDonald and National Geographic Channel. [online] Available at: http://embryo.asu.edu/pages/national-geographic-channels-womb, accessed 4 April 2015.

Macintyre, C and McVitty, K (2004) *Movement and Learning in the Early Years: Supporting Dyspraxia (DCD) and Other Difficulties*. London: Paul Chapman.

Restak, R M (1984) *The Brain*. New York: Bantam.

Samuel, L (n.d.) The brain stem. [online] Available at: www.interactive-biology.com/1835/the-3-parts-of-the-brain-stem-and-their-functions-episode-27/, accessed 4 April 2015.

Stiles, J (2012) Neural Growth and Pruning, in Woodhead, M and Oates, J (eds) *Early Childhood in Focus 7: Developing Brains.* Milton Keynes: Open University.

Stock Kranowitz, C (2003) *The Out-of-Sync Child Has Fun: Activities for Kids with Sensory Processing Disorder*, revised edition. New York: Perigee.

Stock Kranowitz, C. (2005) *The Out-of-Sync Child: Recognizing and Coping with Sensory Processing Disorder*, revised edition. New York: Perigee.

Tallack, P (2006) *In the Womb: Witness the Journey from Conception to Birth through Astonishing 3D Images*. Washington, DC: National Geographic.

2 Early movement and learning development

Key messages

- Early movement is a developmental process that begins in the womb and continues into Key Stage 2 when children are 8–9 years old (Greenland, 2000). It is important to be aware of this in terms of understanding and observation in order to respond positively.

- The engaging in, or experience of, these movements does not always take place in a chronological order, so it is crucial to understand the maturation process to support the revisiting of missed or low levels of movement experiences.

- Children have an innate desire to move. Therefore children's significant movements should be facilitated and supported.

- Children learn through repetition, therefore continuous opportunities for spontaneous movement are an essential and integral part of learning and strengthening of the pathways between the brain and the body (Goddard Blythe, 2005).

- Understanding the clear links between movements and learning development ensures children's individual needs are met and appropriately supported.

- Accurate assessment within the early years should be carried out within an environment that supports the child's physicality.

Introduction: identifying significant movements and understanding impact on learning

This chapter begins to identify specific movements and how the opportunity to continually revisit them throughout the early years has a significant impact on the child's learning development. It is important as you progress through this chapter to look at children's early movements in their purest form and not to link them with a medical diagnosis. It is equally important to respond to observations consistently and not as stand-alone events. Taking an area at a time, the chapter examines how these very simple movements impact and support learning: 'A physically active child is a happy child, and a happy child is a learning child' (Clarke, 2014, p 4).

Floor play

Floor play refers to those early movements when a child is lying on their back and/or their tummy. Regular time spent on the floor in both these positions contributes greatly to a child's development and supports the inhabitation of their primitive reflexes (O'Connor, 2014).

Key learning developments:

- develops self-confidence and awareness of self in space;

- supports head and muscle control;

- control of eye movements/eye hand coordination;

- develops the opening up of the palm of the hand through providing weight-bearing opportunities;

- supports the smooth functioning of the tactile sense.

Self-confidence and awareness of self in space

Whilst on their back it is a natural form of exploration for babies and young children to reach and grab their toes, move from side to side and pull their toes to their mouth. Crucial in developing the proprioception sense, these movements are frequently witnessed, but their importance is sometimes overlooked. This early reaching and grabbing movement provides the baby/child with the information they need to give them the awareness of the ends of their body and build their awareness of self. Babies are not born with a natural sense of where the ends of their body are, so providing floor-based opportunities to play with their hands and feet strongly supports this. This is often referred to as body mapping. 'If the brain does not have accurate "maps" of the body, then it cannot "navigate" or plan body movements' (Ayres, 2005, p 57).

Throughout this process, babies become secure in where they are in relation to the space around them, in turn building self-confidence and independence.

Head and neck control

Opportunities for gaining head control and strengthening the neck muscles are fundamental in providing the early foundations of balance and coordination and the control of eye movements. Where the importance of floor play is recognised within the early months one of two things happens, either the baby rolls over onto or the adult places them on their tummy. For the majority of young babies, having time on their tummy regularly is a positive experience. Whilst in the prone position and before having gained full control, they may lift their heads for a few seconds, in turn developing the neck muscles. Over time this movement becomes stronger and the head is held for longer. The early lifting of the head begins to build the early pathways in the brain supporting the development of the vestibular system and eye tracking. Over time as the body and head move the muscles of both eyes strengthen. This enables focusing and tracking, which is needed for reading (Hannaford, 2005).

Developing the control of eye movements/eye–hand coordination

The asymmetrical tonic neck reflex (as described in Chapter 1) further supports the child's ability to develop control of the eye movements supporting early reaching and grabbing activities (Goddard Blythe, 2008). These early opportunities are supportive of the ongoing development of eye–hand coordination, which plays a vital role in a child's fine motor control.

Open palm

Whilst exploring tummy time a child will begin to open clenched hands. The opening up of the palm and weight-bearing provides opportunities to support the sensory integration system and the development of early mark-making, fine motor skills and dexterity.

Tactile sense

> The tactile system, or sense of touch, plays a major part in determining physical, mental and emotional human behavior. Every one of us, from infancy onward, needs constant tactile stimulation to keep us organised and functioning.
>
> (Stock Kranowitz, 2005, p 82)

Children experience sensory feedback through the soles of their feet, as well as through the palms of their hands. Therefore allowing children to be barefoot is important in providing opportunities to support this (White, 2012). Sensory opportunities support the child to feel comfortable in their body whilst knowing where their body is in space. This is more difficult when their feet are away from the floor. This can often be identified, for example, when children are having dinner, sitting at the table on a chair where their feet don't touch the floor. In searching for a connecting point which enables the sensory feedback system to be stimulated they can be seen to kick out to the side or up to the top of the table. As an early years practitioner it is important to recognise this rather than reprimanding: 'Keep your feet still', 'Stop kicking the table.'

CASE STUDY

Practitioner feedback: 'This absolutely resonated with me …'

Mealtimes had become a challenge, and tired of hearing my own voice repeatedly say 'Keep your feet still', 'Stop kicking' and 'Come and sit back down', I identified and attended a relevant two-day training course. As the tutor addressed the importance of early movement and the sensory feedback system through familiar situations, everything she said absolutely resonated with me. In responding to my specific situation she asked if when the child was sitting on the chair their feet touched the floor. Where the answer was 'no', she made the suggestion of placing a step under the table for the child to rest their feet on. Sceptical that something so simple could reform mealtimes and yet desperate to try anything, I returned home prepared to give it a go. Amazed at the instant response, I went back to the second day of the training only too happy to share the positive transformation that had taken place.

Reflective question

» *Having read the case study, are there other situations that you can think of that you would now perceive and respond to differently?*

Uncomfortable on the tummy

Whilst exploring the benefits of tummy time, you need to be mindful that for some babies, being flat on their tummy is an uncomfortable experience. This is not unusual for those who were premature babies or those with reflux/digestive issues. The use of props such as bolsters or cushions can be helpful. The use of a gym ball may also be helpful in this situation: for young children especially, it can be a more comfortable and fun way to engage in tummy time.

Reflective question

» *Thinking beyond physical reasons, are there other reasons why babies and young children may not experience tummy time? Share your thoughts.*

Crawling (on the tummy)

Crawling and creeping act as integrating experiences in combining the use of several systems involved in motor control: balance, proprioception, vision, and cooperative use of the two sides of the body (bilateral integration) which reflect active use of the two sides of the brain.

(Goddard Blythe, 2008, p 91)

Key learning developments:

* improves physical alignment (neck, shoulders and hips);
* develops posture and balance;
* encourages shoulder, lower-arm rotation and open palm;
* seems to support bladder and bowel control.

Alignment

During crawling, the physical alignment of the neck, shoulders and hips begins to take place. As the opportunity to engage in this movement is perfected over time the ability to move confidently around with a smooth cross-lateral rotation (moving using the opposite arm/leg) is established. The benefit of this smooth rotation becomes evident when a child begins to walk upright showing a well-aligned hip rotation (Greenland, 2000).

Posture and balance

Upright balance begins to be developed whilst on the tummy through early floor-based movements and is not something that is fully learnt whilst in an upright, standing position (Goddard Blythe, 2005).

Crawling continues to build on those early tummy opportunities and the lifting of the head through supporting the development of the proprioception sense, vestibular system and therefore in time upright balance.

Shoulder, lower-arm rotation and open palm

The development of the shoulder, lower arm and open palm through crawling supports the muscle tone and alignment for early writing skills. This is vital, given that it takes the strength and control of over 25 muscles for a child to hold a pencil and write a word (Clarke, 2013). As a practitioner your key question here should be whether you are providing sufficient opportunities to support the maturation process of the physical skills needed to hold a pencil, rather than focusing on simply meeting the Early Learning Goal.

Bladder and bowel control

Time spent on the tummy is thought to help supports bladder and bowel control. 'Time crawling on the tummy makes the child aware of the genital area through ventral stimulation, and helps with on-time toilet training' (Lamont, n.d.).

CASE STUDY

Noah

At the start of the summer term, Noah had just celebrated his fourth birthday. With no known medical conditions, he continued to wet himself two or three times over the course of the week in nursery. On the days he remained dry, he was observed to have engaged in more floor-based tummy activities. After a six-week period of increased opportunities within this area there was a marked improvement, with Noah independently sensing and recognising his need to go to the toilet. He transitioned into Reception, dry throughout the day.

Reflective question

» *Could it be that there is a link between the amounts of early floor-based movement young children are exposed to and the increased numbers of children entering nursery/Reception not yet fully toilet-trained? (JABADAO, 2012).*

Creeping (hands and knees)

Key learning developments:

* crossing the midline;

* balance and coordination;

* smooth body alignment and strength;

* spatial awareness.

Crossing the midline

The left hemisphere of your brain controls the muscles on the right side of your body, and the right hemisphere of your brain controls the muscles on the left side of your body.

Movements that take place whilst a child is crawling and creeping cross-laterally enable advanced development of movement to cross the midline (imaginary line down the middle of the body), with both sides of the brain and body being used. Crossing the midline supports the building of the pathways in the brain supportive of motor and cognitive skills.

The ability to recognise the stages of movement throughout observation and assessment is vital. An example would be where there is an expectation for a child to fasten their shoe laces or eat/cut with a knife and fork. For this task to be carried out easily and comfortably by the child they would need to be demonstrating cross-lateral movements.

Children who have difficulty in crossing their midline may also find aspects of reading and writing difficult

Balance and coordination

Creeping opens up a new dimension of balance as the child begins to move away from the floor. As the sensory integration system is further supported a greater accuracy in balance and coordination is established.

CASE STUDY

Ted

Ted's preferred way of moving as a baby was to bum-shuffle. He did this competently and quickly. Standing with the support of furniture and walking independently had taken place by his first birthday. During his early years he showed very little desire to engage in floor-based movements. On the rare occasion he did so, he was observed to creep laterally (movement using the arm and leg on the same side of the body).

As a teenager Ted reflected and commented that he continued to:

- find it difficult to ride a bike in a straight line;
- feel awkward at sport;
- lack confidence in catching a ball/object;
- be unable to maintain good levels of balance whilst learning to ski.

Reflective question

» *Missed movements as a child can be revisited beyond the maturation process. Can you begin to indentify activities and opportunities within your practice that would see this situation minimised?*

Smooth alignment

Movement on all fours also helps to align the spine at the back of the neck with the sacral region (lower back) in preparation for proper alignment in the upright position.

(Goddard Blythe, 2005 p 185)

Creeping on all fours is also a movement children have an inner drive to revisit. Within early years settings it is common to see children of 3 or 4 years old creeping around the floor. This is usually within the context of an imaginative game, somehow making it a more acceptable way to express themselves. It is normal and yet not always recognised that children, especially around the ages of 3 and 4, have an inner need to revisit creeping for extended periods, furthering the development of connections within the brain. This, alongside an ever-active imagination, can often be observed as having a room full of dogs, cats, tigers and bears!

If you have your own children or have worked within Key Stages 1 and 2 then you will also be familiar with the apparent desire of children to continue to return to creeping. Generally speaking, by this stage the learning environment is full of tables and chairs, with more structured times to 'move' and be physical. So the return to creeping is moved outside during play time, often resulting in scuffed knees or holes in trousers. Whilst it might to tempting to avoid these things, the movement itself continues to support children's development.

Spatial awareness

Crawling and creeping not only support the sense of becoming independent, they enable the child to gain knowledge of the space around them and the ability to begin to judge and perceive distance.

Difficulties in this area can often be identified when you consistently notice that every time a child goes to pick a cup up they accidentally misjudge it and knock it over. A further example could be the child attempting and failing to hang their coat on a peg. In these cases telling a child to 'watch what you're doing' is not always helpful. Observation has shown that in many cases the child knows it is highly likely that they are going to 'miss', so reinforcing this can be counterproductive.

Upright/spinning

Key learning developments:

*   complex balance ability and coordination;
*   eye convergence/eye tracking;
*   strengthening the upper body;
*   cross-lateral movements.

Balance and coordination

Having developed muscular strength in the early months, in turn supporting the upright movements in relation to gravity, the child progresses to movements within the upright position such as walking, running, skipping and hopping. As a result of the ongoing development of accurate sensory feedback through the soles of the feet, the balance receptors are stimulated, in turn supporting the vestibular system and the continuation of balance and coordination.

Eye convergence/tracking

Spinning is not always the easiest movement, but to support spinning is integral to supporting and building a child's eye convergence, eye tracking and pre-reading skills. Perhaps you have observed the reader who stops/starts or the reader who reads a couple of sentences and then jumps few lines even though they can recognise the words separately? Opportunities to spin may strengthen the eye convergence and in turn stimulate a greater ease and flow of the words forming together on the page (Greenland, 2000). The vestibular system is vital to supporting the ability to look at a screen/board and then focus at close range, so the ongoing opportunity for linear and rotary movements is essential for children throughout the early years.

Strengthening the upper body

The need for children to support their upper body is often seen when children hang off door handles, swing on curtains or throw their arms around an adult and hang freely. Whilst in no way promoting swinging from door handles, it is important to understand these behaviours do underpin the desire to develop upper-body strength as an essential mechanism that supports the child in being able to maintain good upright positioning and fee comfortable within their bodies.

Reflect here on how you would positively seek to support these behaviours.

CASE STUDY

Evie

Evie is a sociable child who is settled within nursery. As the class gather for a story on the carpet, Evie positions herself away from the group, sitting with her back resting against the wall. When asked to join the group, Evie reluctantly moves forwards. Throughout the story, she is observed to be leaning forwards and resting on the child seated in front of her. When asked to 'sit up and listen', she appears to become distracted by her own socks and shoes. In the group time that follows, Evie finds it difficult to remember the detail of the story.

Reflective question

» *How can you ease the tension between a child being physically comfortable during learning and issues of conformity?*

Cross-lateral movements

Upright movements such as climbing, hopping and kicking are all cross-lateral movements that continue to support connections between both hemispheres of the brain, enabling both sides of the body to work together. In turn, children are able to coordinate their body well in space and move smoothly around in the space available to them.

CASE STUDY

A parent's perspective

Joseph is our second child, who at 2½ years old had confidently reached all his expected milestones and had started to show a real love for playing with Lego bricks. It became noticeable to us at that time that he continued to frequently mouth and chew objects. In nursery, his love for Lego continued, along with his desire to play repeatedly in sand, water, dough and clay. He would play alone and chose not to participate in group activities. His movement was often described to us as clumsy, as he would often trip up and knock things over.

During his time in Reception, we received weekly reports regarding his behaviour, such as that Joseph:

- will sit with his hands over his ears during large-group activities;
- appears overwhelmed and confused;
- is easily distracted;
- finds it difficult to conform to work and complete tasks;
- becomes distressed if his collar and socks are not positioned exactly right;
- needs to constantly have something to touch.

As these behaviours continued into Years 1 and, 2 and given the more formal learning environment, IEPs (individual education plans) were set around completing writing quickly and engaging in activities without fiddling. These were reflected in the reward charts that were used throughout the day.

As parents we obviously wanted the best for our child so we made holistic changes at home, which included:

- giving extended amounts of time for physical activity;
- inviting friends for tea to support his social skills in a quieter environment;
- arranging for a one-to-one tutor, again enabling him to work in a quieter environment and not 'fall behind';
- giving clear instructions in advance, as a change to the routine could cause distress;
- providing calming activities before he went to school (Lego and modelling clay);
- making changes to his diet.

During his time in Years 3 and 4 significant improvements were made in his concentration, engagement in learning and socialising with other children. Whilst it has been a distressing journey for all of us, Joseph is now in Year 5 and, having just attended parents' evening, we were encouraged and proud to hear that he is expected to achieve 'above-average' in all areas of learning.

Reflective questions

»   *Whilst it is clearly important that there is a consistent approach at home and within the setting it is also acknowledged that there will be noticeable differences in environment. How would you have ensured consistency given these differences? Explain your answer.*

»   *Consider the effectiveness of reward charts for a child's development. What would your response have been in this situation? Share your thoughts.*

»   *As a practitioner looking to structure Joseph's school day, are there times that you feel would be more beneficial for him to engage in writing activities?*

»   *Given that it would be inaccurate to say that levels of intelligence are based on the time it takes to complete an activity/piece of work, how would you provide an enabling environment that recognised and supported this?*

Observation, recording and assessment

Observation is at the heart of effective early years provision. 'Accurate observations and assessments form the foundations for all effective early years practice' (Kamen, 2013, p 2).

Alongside daily observation and recording tools, in the area of learning through movement the well-being and involvement scales (Ferre Laevers; Laevers and Heylen, 2004) can be incredibly helpful, and may be something you wish to explore and consider.

Whilst carrying out assessment there is a need to be continually mindful of the enabling environment. As an example, I was asked to work with a local primary school to support them in raising levels in literacy. While reflecting on the most recent GLD (Good Level of Development) scores, what came to light was a low level of achievement in physical development. We created opportunities for lots of spontaneous movement and identified and observed the children who found it difficult to sit up for any extended period of time. What followed was insightful for the team. When children were given permission to complete tasks while lying on the floor on their tummies, what had previously taken a significant amount of time to complete whilst sitting was accomplished in significantly less time. This had the result of revealing previous assessments recording tasks which a child 'could not do' to be inaccurate.

CASE STUDY

George

George is an articulate 5-year-old child who is incredibly creative at capturing his imaginative thoughts and ideas through various means. Every day he demonstrates a curiosity to further explore and develop this. His visual movements demonstrate an innate desire to actively move around with materials and to explore, position and build. In gathering his tools for the day he actively finds a space in which he has the freedom to stand, stretch, lie down and roll.

Yet when George is asked to sit on his chair at a table and engage in a literacy activity, there is a change in his whole demeanour. He is uneasy positioning his body and begins to rock back and forth on his chair. He tucks one leg under his bottom to further support himself and the need to rock builds. The practitioner asks him to stop rocking on his chair. His focus changes to meeting the verbal request of the adult, which brings a level of completion to the task.

Reflective question

» *Reflecting on your practice, consider whether your assessments about the children in your care are accurate in terms of their capabilities or whether they are in part dependent on the positioning of the child during the assessment. Remember, 'what children can do (rather than what they cannot do) is the starting point of a child's education' (Bruce, 2005, p 214).*

Checklist: key questions for observation

- What do you know about the child's early movement development – history/parent partnership?

- Are you aware of any medical needs that could affect the child's movement?

- Where within the setting does the child enjoy moving?

- Taking lots of observations made over a week, what percentage of time is spent on the floor, crawling and in an upright position?

- When the child is engaged in movement can you identify which stage the child is predominantly moving on?

- At what time of day are they most engaged in learning?

- Whilst engaged in activities, are they displaying high levels of well-being and involvement?

- In what positions do they seem most comfortable?

- What is the child's sensory preference?

- When sitting in a group, how and where does the child choose to position themselves?

- Where do they stand if they are asked to make a line with their peers?

- Do they need to hold on to something to enable them to concentrate and engage?

- Are they comfortable with others in their space?

- For how long are they able to sit upright?

- Are there certain textures that irritate them?

- Do they have a preference for taking off their socks and shoes?

Practical tasks

» *Use the key questions above when observing a cohort of children over a period of time. 'Tuning in' will give you an invaluable insight into how to further support the children (Brodie, 2013).*

» *Taking a current or recent observation format that you have used, consider if this incorporates the monitoring of early movement. If not, how could you revise this?*

Reflective questions

» *Consider the differences between today's society and that of 30 years ago. What impact could they have on children's opportunities to move? List your thoughts.*

» *Thinking about your setting or one you have recently visited, what opportunities are provided to support the maturation process of learning through movement, and do they release the child to comfortably engage in learning?*

» *What might sure foundations for underpinning children's learning through movement in the curriculum look like?*

» *Thinking about your recent experience in practice, were your verbal requests in alignment with your understanding of the child's physical development? Try to give some examples.*

» *All children are unique and begin to walk at different ages. Yet the question 'are they not walking yet?' when they reach their first birthday, can still often be heard. How would you respond to hearing this question?*

» *Consider your setting in relation to the prime areas of development. Is every child given the opportunity and right to be seen and heard at any given time?*

Summary

We have a brain because we have a motor system that allows us to move away from danger and towards opportunity. Educational systems that reduce most student movement to one appendage, writing sequences of letters and digits on a playing field the size of a sheet of paper don't understand the significance of motor development.

Robert Sylvester (taken from Hannaford, 2005, p 107)

This chapter has demonstrated the links between movement and learning and explored some familiar scenarios within the early years. As the importance of physical development within the early years has been increasingly highlighted in recent years, you need to be ever mindful that you are providing an enabling environment and must have the depth of understanding to support these vital early movements and learning.

What you know and what you can offer the youngest children in your care have to work hand in hand.

Further reading

The following books are suggested to give you further insight into the importance of movement and sensory integration and its vital role in learning. They will support you with the links between the theory and your practice whilst offering you practical activities.

Ayres, A J (2005) *Sensory Integration and the Child: Understanding Hidden Sensory Challenges*, 25th anniversary edition. Los Angeles: Western Psychological Services.

Goddard Blythe, S (2005) *The Well Balanced Child: Movement and Early Learning*, revised edition. Stroud, Gloucestershire: Hawthorn Press.

Hannaford, C. (2005) *Smart Moves: Why Learning Is Not All in Your Head*, 2nd edition. Salt Lake City, UT: Great River Books.

Stock Kranowitz, C (2003) *The Out-of-Sync Child Has Fun: Activities for Kids with Sensory Processing Disorder*, revised edition. New York: Perigee.

Stock Kranowitz, C (2005) *The Out-of-Sync Child: Recognizing and Coping with Sensory Processing Disorder*, revised edition. New York: Perigee.

References

Ayres, A J (2005) *Sensory Integration and the Child: Understanding Hidden Sensory Challenges*, 25th anniversary edition. Los Angeles: Western Psychological Services.

Brodie, K (2013) *Observation, Assessment and Planning in the Early Years: Bringing It All Together*. Maidenhead, Berkshire: Open University Press.

Bruce, T (2005) *Early Childhood Education*, 3rd edition. London: Hodder Education.

Clarke, J (2013) Let Them Run and Jump before They Write. *Early Years Update*, 110, July/August 2013, Optimus Education.

Clarke, J (2014) Physical Activities to Underpin PSED. *Early Years*, June 2014, Optimus Education.

Goddard Blythe, S (2005) *The Well Balanced Child: Movement and Early Learning*, revised edition. Stroud, Gloucestershire: Hawthorn Press.

Goddard Blythe, S (2008) *What Babies and Children Really Need*. Stroud, Gloucestershire: Hawthorn Press.

Greenland, P (2000) *Hopping Home Backwards: Body Intelligence and Movement Play*. Leeds: JABADAO Centre for Movement Studies.

Hannaford, C (2005) *Smart Moves: Why Learning Is Not All in Your Head*, 2nd edition. Salt Lake City, UT: Great River Books.

JABADAO (2012) Continence issues. [online] Available at: www.jabadao.org/?blog=blogs/arch-ive/2012/06/17/continence.issues.aspx, accessed 30 March 2015.

Kamen, T (2013) *Observation and Assessment for the EYFS.* London: Hodder Education.

Laevers, F and Heylen, L (2004) *Involvement of Children and Teacher Style: Insights from an International Study on Experiential Education.* Leuven, Belgium: Leuven University Press. [In addition you may also find the following link helpful: www.earlylearninghq.org.uk/earlylearning-hq-blog/the-leuven-well-being-and-involvement-scales/, accessed 30 March 2015.]

Lamont, B (n.d.) The belly crawl. [online] Available at: www.developmentalmovement.org/upload/The%20Belly%20Crawl.pdf, accessed 30 March 2015.

O'Connor, A (2014) First Moves. *Nursery World*, 3–16 November 2014.

Stock Kranowitz, C (2005) *The Out-of-Sync Child: Recognizing and Coping with Sensory Processing Disorder*, revised edition. New York: Perigee.

White, J (2012) Natural play: It's spring now – why not think about going barefoot! [online] Available at: www.janwhitenaturalplay.wordpress.com/natural-play-philosophy-approach/, accessed 30 March 2015.

3 Early movement and the enabling environment

Key messages

- Movement provision is as important as all other areas.

- It is important that a child's innate desire to move is facilitated within daily provision. Therefore offering a wide spectrum of opportunities both indoors and outside is essential.

- Given that movement and key learning take place both on and away from the floor, ensuring that movement spaces are both inviting and appropriate is crucial.

- Understanding the adult role within provision provides a consistent and measured response to a child's individual needs.

- The ability to make reference to the current government framework supports a holistic approach.

Introduction

Movement is an integral part of life from the moment of conception until death, and a child's experience of movement will play a pivotal part in shaping his personality, his feelings, and his achievements. Learning is not just about reading, writing and maths. These are higher abilities that are built upon the integrity of the relationship between brain and body.

(Goddard Blythe, 2005, p 5)

This practical chapter will give you the opportunity to explore how you can effectively offer movement opportunities within your setting, responding to children's individual needs and enable them to positively manage risk.

Developing movement provision

Movement play places a clear emphasis on spontaneity and on child-centred learning, but it requires a high degree of background organisation from adults.
(Greenland, 2000, p 127)

The early years environment is full of activity, with unique individuals who have an innate desire to express themselves through various means of communication.

Through observation you will notice that there is a hub of intrinsic and complex movements. This might include sudden explosions of tipping, tilting and spinning, the curiosity to want to carry out a task walking backwards and the desire to slither under the table on the belly. Facilitated well, these movements provide endless possibilities for discovery, exploration and learning.

Given that children have an innate desire and drive to wire up and connect their brain through movement, how does this translate into the enabling environments on a daily basis?

As children move all the time, it would be true to say that movement is taking place across all areas of provision. However, giving specific movement spaces within which children can safely engage in spontaneous movement activities has a profound and significant impact on their learning.

Construction, sand, water, home and book areas have been familiar features of provision for many years, with much gross motor development facilitated outside or in hall time. So what could an effective indoor movement space look like and what is its purpose?

Offering specific movement spaces will enable you as a practitioner to positively 'signpost' children to a safe and appropriate place to explore and learn and could offer a positive solution to the familiar requests to 'Please stop crawling and get up and walk, people will trip over you', and 'Stop spinning, you will fall over and bump your head on the table.'

Indoor movement spaces

Carefully planned spaces/areas are instrumental in supporting children's early movement development. They communicate to the child that their movement is an important part of their learning (Greenland, 2000). Having identified the importance of early movement in previous chapters, then, planning and providing for them will provide a solid base for learning to take place.

Setting up a space

Principles such as role modelling, introducing resources gradually and responding to children's needs should be applied to setting up an indoor movement space as with any new provision.

Key practical factors to be taken into consideration include:

- identifying the location;
- appropriate lighting/flooring;

- size of the area and the number of children;

- resourcing the area;

- links to mark-making opportunities;

- links to Personal, Social and Emotional Development (PSED) – being seen and heard.

The application of these criteria should be consistent across all ages within early years and they can be enhanced and developed in response to children's specific interests.

Location

Identifying where the movement space would be best placed within the setting is important. It should be a clearly defined space positioned away from direct walk-through areas to the side or corner of the room, supporting the need to move freely without unnecessary disturbance and distraction.

Lighting

Thought should be given to ensuring that the lighting is appropriate for when children are engaged in floor-based movements on their backs. This will ensure that a premature exit from the movement doesn't take place. Drapes/canopies to soften the lighting might offer an effective solution.

Surfaces

Given that floor-based movements are an essential part of establishing and securing pathways in the lower part of the brain, careful consideration needs to be given to ensuring that the enabling environment is supportive of all early movements. For this reason facilitating a space with both a soft and firmer/smooth surface will support both back and tummy movements.

Resources

Table 3.1 gives examples of equipment that can be used, along with some of the benefits which you may like to consider when developing movement space, all of which can be sourced from educational suppliers and JABADAO.

Music

Whilst there is clearly a place for action songs and rhymes within early years, it is important that when working with a movement approach the opportunity for movement is as innate as possible, therefore ensuring that the words of any music do not influence the spontaneous flow.

If music is to be used to support movement, then a range of instrumental pieces from which children can select should be offered. Table 3.2 provides some suggestions.

Table 3.1 Resources list

Resources	Supports
Larger pieces of equipment	
Bolster cushions/gym ball	Tummy play, proprioception and vestibular sense
Balancing/wobble boards	Balance/coordination, upper-body strength and vestibular system
Spinning tops/rockers	Spinning, eye convergence, balance and coordination and vestibular system
Tactile stepping discs	Balance/coordination, sensory feedback and proprioception
Tunnels	Crawling, creeping and proprioception
Smaller pieces of equipment	
Elastic rings	Pushing/pulling, upper-body strength and vestibular system
Lycra material	Eye tracking, pushing/pulling, rocking and vestibular system
Koosh balls	Sensory feedback, tactile sense and eye tracking
Bean bags	Sensory feedback, tactile sense and eye tracking
Ribbon sticks	Wrist, elbow and shoulder pivots and proprioception
Sensory massagers	Sensory feedback system, tactile sense and proprioception

Table 3.2 Musical resources

Title of CD	Type of music
A Jig and a Caper – JABADAO	Upbeat
Out the Gap – Sharon Shannon	Upbeat
The Very Best of Scott Joplin – Scott Joplin	Upbeat
Still Waters – JABADAO	Relaxation
Lazy Days – Stuart Jones	Relaxation
Caribbean Hits – Calypso Steel Band	Relaxation

As every setting is different in shape and size, there is no one fixed way to set up and present a movement space. Remaining mindful of supporting children's individual needs is crucial, and whilst the pictures in Figures 3.1 and 3.2 provide ideas you may wish to use, there may be times that a designated space with no equipment is equally appropriate.

Figures 3.1 and 3.2 *Examples of indoor movement spaces.*

CASE STUDY

The impact of establishing indoor movement spaces

Following the introduction of movement spaces to nursery, Reception and Year 1 and through ongoing observation and assessment, the school reported significant changes in three areas:

1. behaviour – children were calmer indoors and showed improved concentration;

2. gross and fine motor skills – levels of attainment were higher than previous years;

3. well-being and involvement scales – there was a marked improvement, particularly for children with English as an additional language (EAL).

Reflective question

» *Thinking about a setting that you have spent time in, what indoor opportunities were given to children to spontaneously move? How did these indoor opportunities compare with those offered outside? Give examples for both.*

Structured activities

Whilst recognising the importance for ongoing spontaneous movement for a large percentage of time, there is – in moderation – a place for age-appropriate structured and group movement-based activities. These can be a starting point for children and naturally support language and communication and PSED. Using some of the pieces of equipment listed previously, Table 3.3 shows some examples of activities. These are by no means the only ones and children will very quickly create their own.

CASE STUDY

Circle time

For many years I would facilitate circle time, encouraging and recognising the importance of PSED and turn-taking. Moving round the circle maintaining the same direction, the children were given the opportunity to move in the activity. Having attended a training course where the tutor applied the same principle and finding myself positioned as one of the last in the circle, I observed my thoughts to be focused on 'what I was going to do' when it was my turn. Realising that I had given very little thought to what anyone else had done, I began to reflect on this. Acknowledging the degree of the apprehension I felt and the lack of information from others I had taken in formed my new approach to circle time. What became apparent very quickly were higher levels of well-being and involvement.

Table 3.3 Examples of structured movement activities

Resource: large elastic ring
Focus: being seen and heard
Activity: The elastic has the potential to support a whole range of movements on different levels. Working with an individual child or with a group using the elastic offers opportunity for children to initiate how they would like to move and for their movement to be mirrored back to them (Greenland, 2000).

Table 3.3 (Cont.)

Resource: lycra material
Focus: eye tracking/pre-reading
Activity: Having allowed the children to explore, pull, stretch the Lycra, pass each child a Koosh ball. After giving time for sensory feedback ask the children to place the balls on the Lycra before beginning to lift the Lycra and make the balls jump.   Be mindful that until children have developed vertical tracking it is highly likely that they will track the ball going up but find it difficult to track it coming back down, often resulting in children looking quickly in all directions to try relocate the ball. This again emphasises the importance of ensuring that verbal requests are developmentally appropriate. Slower-moving resources such as balloons or a beach ball can also be helpful in supporting the development of eye tracking.

Resource: parachute
Focus: rolling
Activity: Rolling not only supports proprioception, balance and coordination, it also is a self-soothing movement enabling children to connect with themselves. Whilst working towards rolling in a straight line children veer off to the left and right. Giving opportunity for children to roll across the parachute whilst creating gentle waves offers an open space with a safe and defining edge to give the child a sense of where their body is in relation to the space around them.

Reflective questions

Acknowledging that turn-taking remains important and that all children have the right to be seen and heard both verbal and non-verbally, reflect on your practice in relation to facilitating circle time and group activities.

» *What do you currently do?*

» *Are there any changes that you would consider making?*

CASE STUDY

Incorporating movement in PE sessions

Having attended training and supported the establishing of movement spaces throughout nursery and Reception I made the decision to incorporate early movement within PE.

The first step was changing the first ten minutes of every PE lesson to allow children to move in any way they wanted, along with the introduction of a relaxation time at the end of each lesson.

Having implemented these changes, a further decision was made to introduce movement PE lessons offering a range of equipment such as Lycra, play mats, scarves, ribbons and foam balls which were made available for the children to explore.

After observing the children over a period of six weeks:

- levels of well-being and involvement in these sessions were significantly higher than in normal PE lessons;

- children who were quiet and reserved grew in confidence;

- there was a desire from the children to rehearse what they had done in the sessions back in class;

- they talked about PE in a way they had not previously done and actively planned what they were going to do in the following week's session.

Reflective questions

»   *How would you ensure that early movement is incorporated into PE lessons on a regular basis? Outline your ideas in detail.*

»   *Given the need for children to process their experiences, how could you ensure that this was facilitated?*

Children need time to 'process' their experiences, just as we do. It is this reflective activity that generates an internal locus of control, and a sense of empowerment. It also enables children – and adults – to develop a sense of purpose.

(Roberts, 2010, p 69)

Movement within home-based and group settings

It is important for settings to offer effective movement experiences supporting children and their families. The principles are of course the same and the impact equally significant.

CASE STUDY

A parent's view of learning through a movement group

I received information about and then took my 2 year-old daughter to a 'children's learning through movement' group at the local children's centre. My daughter thoroughly enjoyed her time there, exploring a range of movement equipment and engaging in large creative and sensory floor-based activities. The open-ended resources supported her repeated desire to be 'enveloped' in varying ways (Featherstone and Louis, 2013). Having attended weekly for a six-week period I came away not only with a more in-depth knowledge and understanding of the importance of early movement, but also a growing sense that this was an intrinsic part of my daughter's development that could support her in her reading and writing. These significant movements became incorporated into activities and ongoing opportunities at home. Having just received her SAT results at the end of year we celebrated her 2a (higher than expected) in writing and 3c (exceeding expectation) in reading. Whilst acknowledging that there are many aspects that contribute to children attaining high levels of reading and writing, as a parent I believe the early movement experiences were fundamental.

Reflective questions

» *Given that the maturation period for early movement is 0–8 years old, how can you ensure that these key messages are effectively shared with parents/carers within group settings?*

» *Identify the key messages and benefits that you would endeavour to include.*

CASE STUDY

A parent's perspective: Rashmi

Born on her due date, Rashmi was diagnosed as having hip displacement. She was a sociable little character who successfully reached all her early milestones. At 11 months, she received treatment in hospital for her condition. Following her time in hospital, she grew noticeably quiet in the company of others, and avoided social situations. By the time she reached 24 months, she was reluctant to communicate with others outside her immediate family. At home, Rashmi experienced lots of opportunities to engage in floor play and experienced lots of physical and sensory activities. At nursery, we were invited to join a six-week movement play programme for families. As the weeks progressed, her confidence grew and in the later sessions she started to participate fully. It was evident that during the movement sessions she felt more relaxed. This was noticeable in her posture, gestures, facial expression and confidence in accessing the equipment and activities. Although she was still verbally quiet during the early sessions, she communicated clearly through her physical movements. Mid-way through the programme, and following the opportunity to move spontaneously, she occasionally started to speak. This was such a big step forwards for her. After the programme finished, the nursery setting continued to support her through providing movement spaces and opportunities. Rashmi continues to progress at her own pace through all areas of learning. Over time she has found her voice and her inner confidence. She has grown to be a very well-respected, active pupil at school and is making excellent progress in her personal sports activities. Movement play has been fundamental in my little girl's development and has been embryonic in enabling her to be the person she is today.

Reflective question

» *Having read the case study and giving careful thought to children's well-being, are there aspects of your practice that you would seek to change? Explain and give reasons for your answer.*

CASE STUDY

Childminder's feedback

Having child-minded for a number of years I had frequently heard myself saying 'Stop running around the coffee table, you will fall and bump your head.' This, along with having to manage the children's less than willing response to cooperate with my instruction, was at times frustrating. It wasn't until I gained understanding on the innate response to run, and run in circles, that I readdressed the positioning of the furniture in my home to both support and encourage what I now knew the children needed.

Reflective question

»   What suggestions would you offer a home/home-based setting on providing movement opportunities indoors?

Outdoor movement provision

The development of gross motor skills is often associated with the outdoors, with time, for example, for running, skipping and jumping to take place. However, there may be an assumption that in being outside children will naturally do all that they need to do physically. As a practitioner you will need to give careful thought to your outdoor provision so that it will enable children to learn, enjoy and reach their potential (Bilton, 2014).

Figure 3.3 An example of an outdoor movement space within the wider outdoor provision.

CASE STUDY

Monkey bars

Samuel is in foster care and is '[failing] to thrive'. He has been attending the children's centre five full days a week for three and a half years.

Samuel spends a large proportion of his time outside. He started exploring the monkey bars when he moved into Foundation Stage, and would stand on the platform and reach for the bars. Unable to reach them, he would call for support from his key person. He would hang from them for a few seconds before letting go.

After months of practice, persistence, precision and determination, Samuel had grown in confidence. His arms had grown long enough to enable him to reach the first bar, making him more independent. In between spending time on the monkey bars, Samuel would run around the garden, roll down the hill, spin in the cone, dance in the home corner, ride around on the tricycle and topple over in the movement area. He was a very active and confident mover.

When Samuel was nearly 4 years old he succeeded. He was able to hang from the bars, pull his feet up, hook his knees over the bars and drop his upper body down. He could hang upside down and move across the bars one at a time.

Reflective question

» *How could time spent on the monkey bars support a child with the more formal learning that will take place indoors as they move through the education system? Explain your answer.*

Given that some children at home and in pre-school settings spend so much of their time outdoors, it is vital for children to be supported in all areas of learning outdoors.

Outdoor provision must support inclusion and meet the needs of individuals, offering a diverse range of play-based experiences.

(Warden, 2012, p 16)

Movements such as running, rolling, pushing, pulling, climbing and jumping all support the proprioception sense (O'Connor, 2012) and remain strong innate desires within young children. Hopping and skipping support balance and coordination and cognitive development whilst supporting the connections in the brain.

Reflecting on outdoor provision that you have recently seen as part of your practice, ask yourself if children have had opportunities to engage in all aspects of movement. Given the opportunity, what enhancements would you make to further develop this area of learning?

Risk is a part of life: 'The willingness to take risks is also an important learning disposition' (Tovey, 2011, p 87). 'Having a go' and taking on a challenge play a positive role in self-confidence and well-being.

Taking into consideration the culture of risk assessment, are you also confident that with support your outdoor opportunities offer all the movement experiences children need?

The role of the adult and a shared ethos

The role of the early years practitioner is crucial in supporting a child's spontaneous movement.

A practitioner should:

- value movement;
- provide safe spaces for children to move spontaneously as their body directs them;
- engage in and be comfortable with movement conversations;
- observe, record and monitor a child's learning through movement;
- be a role model;
- offer a range of sensory opportunities;
- ensure a wide range of equipment is available to support all aspects of movement;
- share information and opportunities with colleagues/families;
- plan appropriate activities;
- provide mark-making opportunities following movement conversations;
- enjoy and celebrate movement.

The importance of mirroring

Being seen, heard and valued is an empowering experience. The percentage of communication deemed non-verbal communication varies depending on research: 'Most non-verbal communication is through our bodies' (Bruce, 2004, p 75). What is important here is the response to the child and the skill of the practitioner in making such responses (Chilvers, 2006). Mirroring in its simplest form is 'copying what another is doing'. If this is applied to children's early movements, the term 'movement conversation' is sometimes used.

During a movement conversation you should closely observe and respond to all body movements, large and small, breathing, gestures, facial expressions, timing and energy levels.

Having acknowledged that movement is a way of communicating and is a child's first language, it is therefore essential that you can effectively engage in a movement conversation with a child. It is also recognised to be the language children refer back to when they don't have the words.

Movement conversations can happen anywhere and not just in a designated movement space. They can involve the individuals in close proximity or at a distance across the room.

Points to be mindful of during movement conversations:

*   allow yourself to connect with the conversation before trying to process it;

*   maintain a safe environment;

*   ensure enough time for your conversation;

*   keep verbal communication to an absolute minimum;

*   listen and respond to all movements;

*   ensure that you support the child in bringing the conversation to an end. If appropriate you may want to take the conversation down towards the floor or make the movements smaller before finally separating from each other.

CASE STUDY

William's movement conversation

William is 4 years old and has been attending the children's centre since he was 1 year old. He loves the opportunity to participate in group movement sessions and is always one of the first in the line. Movement conversations are a familiar language for him. This session was no different and he eagerly came into the room. Following opportunities to move spontaneously using a variety of equipment, the session moved into a time of relaxation before ending. All the children chose a coloured scarf. In a way that was significantly out of character, William grabbed the blue scarf. As the children began to relax, William lay face down, still, and quietly began to cry into his blue scarf. With no words spoken, a hand was gently placed on his back. The other children ended the session and left the room. William remained still with his head slightly turned to the side. Lying next to William and sensing that words would be an intrusion at that point, eye contact was made. What followed was a very gentle and yet powerful movement conversation in which William initiated the movement. As the conversation came to a close, William began to share. He had regularly stayed at his grandad's house at weekends. Recently his grandad had died. William shared that when he stayed at grandad's house he had a blue duvet, and he was missing him lots.

Reflective question

» *Reflect on a situation where a movement conversation may have been the most appropriate response. Give details and explain your thinking.*

Consistency from adults for children is essential. You should therefore take time to think about those aspects that you believe are fundamental in developing a shared ethos about movement within your setting. The list below may help you in exploring this.

- Movement is a language.

- Movement is a key and fundamental way in which children learn.

- All children have the right to be seen and heard.

- Enabling environments are essential in supporting development.

- Shared understanding within the setting of the links between movement, sensory integration and the brain is essential for consistency.

Reflective questions

Consider the importance of having a shared ethos in relation to early movement.

» *How might this benefit the setting and the children?*

» *Highlight the key factors that you would propose as part of a shared ethos.*

Emotional development

Babies express their emotions through physical movements. It is only with the attention of a companionable adult who is able to listen deeply to what the young child is trying to communicate that they can begin the long process of self regulation.

Kinaesthetically, young children are able to immerse themselves in a world of emotion and can be supported to express emotion through movement, colour, sound and music. If they are feeling sad, angry, disappointed or joyful, movement enables them to communicate their feelings in a way that is more natural for some than verbalising their emotions.

A gate towards inclusion or a barrier towards exclusion?
Sir Ken Robinson, an author, speaker and international advisor on education in the arts to government, completes his presentation on TED (2006), How Schools Kill Creativity, with a personal story about Gillian Lynne. Lynne, a British ballerina, theatre director and famous choreographer for musicals such as Cats and The Phantom of the Opera, was being interviewed by Robinson. Robinson wanted to know how she had discovered her talent. From as early as she could remember, she danced. At school her movement was perceived as disruptive and she was sent to see a doctor. Gillian's mother explained her daughter's difficulties while Gillian sat on her hands and tried to listen. After a while, the doctor told Gillian that he wanted to speak to her mother in private. As he left the room, he turned the radio on. He then encouraged her mother to watch. Gillian began to dance. The doctor turned to Gillian's mother and told her that there was nothing wrong with Gillian. He told her mother to take her to a dance school. Gillian remembers how she suddenly felt 'at home' amongst others who learned primarily through their bodies.

(Vine, 2011, p 35)

Reflective question

» *How could you ensure that the needs of children who primarily learn and express themselves in this way are met? Give examples.*

Embedding a movement play approach

Careful thought and planning is needed to ensure effective movement provision within settings.

CASE STUDY

Acknowledging that physical development was important and yet curious to gain an increased knowledge of 'why' children need to move in specific ways, all of our early years staff attended appropriate training.

Our school development plan was focusing on closing gaps for pupil premium (in school) and for all children in the bottom 20 per cent across school.

Last year the school had ten children in the bottom 20 per cent leaving Reception. Wanting to see this number reduced, we felt that initial movement sessions with the children in both nursery and Reception, with a view to embedding a movement play approach, would greatly help the current children identified as being in our school's bottom 20 per cent to develop their 'readiness to learn' across all areas of the curriculum.

A series of spontaneous and structured sessions for every child in both nursery and Reception was delivered by an experienced early years movement practitioner. This offered insight and gave perspective in responding to individual needs and identifying and providing ongoing opportunities.

Enhancements to both the indoor and outdoor areas were made. Movement spaces within nursery and Reception were identified indoors, with staff feeling confident in responding to what they observed. Outdoors saw defined areas created for large-scale movement away from bikes and other equipment. Large-scale mark-making through various means was provided and ensured that movement was valued and supported across all activities.

A training/workshop was offered to all parent/carers of children in the nursery and Reception giving an opportunity to hear key messages and engage in and experience early movements, with ideas and suggestions to support movement at home.

Having completed moderation and received final data reports we recognised the positive impact that introducing a movement approach has had in our setting: we have one child in the bottom 20 per cent this year compared with ten last year. In the EYFSP (Early Years Foundation Stage Profile) setting, boys' and girls' average point scores were higher than local authority and national results in every area of learning. We are so proud of the work that we have done and the huge impact that it has had on the children. We are committed to continue to develop this approach within our setting.

Reflective question

» *How would you ensure that all children in your setting have all the movement opportunities they need to develop their 'readiness to learn' across all areas of the curriculum? Give examples.*

Practical task

» *Focusing on a setting that you have previously worked in or are currently working in, give thought to how you could develop a resource supporting the sharing of information with staff and families on the importance of movement provision. Provide as much detail as possible in your answer.*

Reflective questions

» *From your experience, is the indoor movement space given the same credibility as other areas of provision? If not, why not?*

» *Taking the time period of a week, what percentage of your response to children's spontaneous movement is supported through mirroring?*

» *How would you ensure that a child who chose to spend very little time in the movement space had opportunity to explore their early significant movements?*

» *Explain how you would support schematic learning through movement (Atherton and Nutbrown, 2013). Having considered the importance of movement spaces and the need for children to move freely, identify how you would respond to and support the following children:*

1. C has been attending the setting for six months and is familiar with the routine, practitioners and his peers. It has been identified that C is often 'pushing' other children, and practitioners have observed C becoming quite distressed when other children 'crowd' around her.

2. S is a confident little boy who independently selects where and with what he wants to play. He shows an interest in making large circular movements and is often seen trying to maintain balance whilst spinning on the spot. He finds wheels fascinating.

3. M attends nursery three days a week. On arriving, she quickly visits each area of provision, pausing for very short periods of time at each. As she moves around, it is observed that she has a tendency to lean forwards and frequently bumps into the equipment around her.

Summary

Watching a child makes it obvious that the development of his mind comes through his movements.

Montessori (n.d.)

The chapter has shown the importance of movement provision, both indoors and out, while offering guidance and suggestions on how to implement, develop and use spaces with a range of resources that support physical development. It has been mindful throughout that movement is a child's first language (Goddard Blythe, 2008) and has emphasised connections with PSED. As the three prime areas of the EYFS are an integral part of children's early movement planning, observation and assessment should reflect this.

> *If you plan activities for physical development, then you are planning for all three prime areas at the same time.*
>
> (Clarke, 2014, p 4)

Further reading

The following book and article are suggested to give you further perspective and understanding on the importance of movement provision within the early years. They will allow you to continue to explore key learning whilst offering practical activities and suggestions.

Greenland, P (2000) *Hopping Home Backwards: Body Intelligence and Movement Play*. Leeds: JABADAO Centre for Movement Studies.

Nursery World (2012) Nursery Equipment. *Nursery World, Supplement: Physical Development Special*, May 2012.

References

Atherton, F and Nutbrown, C (2013) *Understanding Schemas and Young Children: From Birth to Three*. London: Sage.

Bilton, H (2014) *Playing Outside: Activities, Ideas and Inspiration for the early years*, 2nd edition. Abingdon: Routledge.

Bruce, T (2004) *Developing Learning in Early Childhood: 0–8 years*. London: Sage.

Chilvers, D (2006) *Young Children Talking: The Art of Conversation and Why Children Need to Chatter*. London: Early Education: The British Association for Early Childhood Education.

Clarke, J (2014) Physical Activities to Underpin PSED. *Early Years*, June 2014, Optimus Education.

Featherstone, S and Louis, S (2013) *Understanding Schemas in Young Children: Again! Again!*, 2nd edition. London: Bloomsbury/Featherstone Education.

Goddard Blythe, S (2005) *The Well Balanced Child: Movement and Early Learning*, revised edition. Stroud, Gloucestershire: Hawthorn Press.

Goddard Blythe, S. (2008) *What Babies and Children Really Need*. Stroud, Gloucestershire: Hawthorn Press.

Greenland, P (2000) *Hopping Home Backwards: Body Intelligence and Movement Play*. Leeds: JABADAO Centre for Movement Studies.

Montessori, M (n.d.) Daily Montessori. [online] Available at: www.dailymontessori.com/maria-montessori-quotes/, accessed 30 March 2015.

O'Connor, A (2012) A Clean Sweep. *Nursery World, Supplement: Physical Development Special*, May 2012.

Roberts, R (2010) *Wellbeing from Birth*. London: Sage.

Tovey, H (2011) Achieving the Balance: Challenge, Risk and Safety, in White, J (ed.) *Outdoor Provision in the Early Years*. London: Sage.

Vine, P (2011) *A Journey from Within*. Leeds: Leeds City Council.

Warden, C (2012) *Nurture through Nature*, 2nd edition. Crieff, Perthshire: Mindstretchers.

4 Early movement and supporting writing

Key messages

- Motor development and sensory integration are fundamental in supporting early writing.

- Children need to develop physically, and have the strength and control over their muscles in order to sit comfortably and write with a pencil.

- Movement opportunities that support mark-making and early writing should take place across all areas of provision.

- An understanding of the importance of language is crucial in the development of writing.

- Practitioners should value and empower children in the process of becoming 'writers'.

Introduction

Identifying what needs to take place within the body to strengthen and support muscle control is fundamental in addressing the question of how to support young children in their early writing. You need to be confident in your understanding and creative in providing quality provision.

Within the EYFS framework, Physical Development: Moving and Handling, the Early Learning Goal (ELG) states:

> Children show good control and co-ordination in large and small movements. They move confidently in a range of ways, safely negotiating space. They handle equipment and tools effectively, including pencils for writing.

> (Early Education, 2012, p 24)

In supporting children in working towards achieving this goal you need to recognise that the development of large core muscles (for example the neck and back), which in turn support the muscles in the arms and legs and then those of the fingers and toes, is of paramount importance. This will enable you to support children with a good physical foundation, ensuring that they are not prematurely expected to use a pencil (Palmer and Corbett, 2003).

Gross motor skills

Gross motor skill enables and supports the movement of the large muscle groups within the body.

Developing core strength and control is essential in supporting movement (Pape, 2013). This usually comes from the core of the body moving outwards and from the top of the body moving down, initially with control of the head leading to the neck and back muscles. Time in the prone position is beneficial here. Prior to the small muscles in the hands being developed, there is a need to develop the larger muscles in the shoulders and the arms. Again, time spent in the prone position with weight-bearing through the forearms and crawling is supportive of this process. Giving children the freedom to creep strengthens the muscles in both the arms and the legs and, along with rolling, develops balance and coordination.

The upright movements of jumping, hopping, skipping, running and climbing all develop strength, balance and coordination throughout the body, further supporting and enabling the child to be able to sit up correctly (Clarke, 2013).

In the early stages of development, as the core muscles strengthen, early mark-making has the opportunity to emerge. You should aim to provide both vertical and horizontal mark-making opportunities to support the development of the shoulder, elbow and wrist pivots (Bryce Clegg, 2013).

- Shoulder pivot: this can be observed and described as a straight arm with the movement coming from the shoulder, the marks being large vertical, horizontal or circular ones.
- Elbow pivot: this can be observed and described as the elbow beginning to bend and the increased motion of movement in the arm becoming more fluent with an expanding range of vertical, horizontal and circular marks.
- Wrist pivot: as the shoulder becomes stronger at supporting the arm and hand and the elbow becomes more controlled at the side of the body, the wrist pivot can be observed and described as smaller motor movements and greater manipulation, with the mark-making implement resulting in finer marks.

Activities and resources

Table 4.1 offers a range of indoor and outdoor gross motor activities and resources that support children's motor development and sensory integration that are beneficial to early writing. As with any provision, you would need to risk-assess them appropriately.

Table 4.1 Gross motor activities. Gross motor activities develop and strengthen the muscles through large movements, balance and coordination, body awareness and sensory integration

Type of gross motor movement	Suggestions for activities	Suggestions for resources
Tummy/back play	Offer a variety of floor coverings for children to explore. Provide a range of objects to encourage reaching/grabbing. Give opportunities for children to be mobile whilst on their tummy.	Textured materials, bubble wrap, corrugated cardboard. Heuristic/natural resources sensory objects/mobiles, crinkled paper. Large activity balls, bolster cushions, body and balancing boards.
Crawling/creeping	Ensure smooth and other various textured surfaces are available. Offer and encourage children to create crawling/creeping opportunities. Support children in creating their own obstacle courses. Provide large, floor-based creative activities.	Shiny materials. mirror paper, smooth floors, large gym mats, wood chip and natural surfaces. Combat tunnels, cargo nets, tunnels, large boxes, dens and soft play equipment. Cones, hoops, balancing beams and tunnels. Paint, ice, sand and collage.
Rolling	Ensure that there are slopes within your provision for children to explore. Design and create tracks to roll through.	Grass hills, soft play, slopes. Chalks, cones, pieces of material.
Spinning	Offer supportive resources alongside safe spaces to spontaneously spin.	Giant spinning cones/tops, flat spinning discs and mini spinning cones.
Running/skipping/hopping	Give time and space for these three movements to naturally take place and through games, races and stories.	Balls, skipping-ropes and chalks to mark out tracks.
Upright – shoulder rotation	Ensure that children have access to throwing and large shoulder rotation activities.	Balls, nets and target mats. Large ribbon, sticks and flags.

Table 4.1 (cont.)

Type of gross motor movement	Suggestions for activities	Suggestions for resources
Jumping	Provide a variety of jumping experiences and incorporate stories and action songs.	Stepping-stones and tactile discs, crates, hoops, trampolines and examples of books and action songs.
Climbing/hanging	Open-ended resources are beneficial here along with climbing walls and opportunities to hang from monkey bars.	Crates/tyres/planks/tubes, climbing frames, soft play equipment, climbing-walls and monkey bars.
Pushing/pulling/lifting/ strengthening grip	Ensure children have access to a wide range of resources that support these types of movements.	Sweeping brushes, paint rollers, large elastic bands, Lycra material, parachute activities, wheelbarrows, stilts and bikes and scooters.

Fine motor skills

Fine motor skill supports the coordination of the small muscles in the body that can enable tasks to be carried out with accuracy and precision.

Whilst focusing on supporting fine motor development it is important to continue to recognise and link the importance of the gross motor activities to the development and strength of the hand. Lack of hand development can be problematic for children with their early writing. Therefore movement involving hands and knees not only supports the strengthening of the muscles in the upper arm but also the development of the bones in the hand (Hannaford, 2005). This in turn allows weight-bearing whilst continuing to support the development of the full open palm stretch and dexterity.

Most weight-bearing takes place on the little finger side of the hand (Buckner, n.d.). Activities such as pulling and stretching, climbing, hanging, time spent on the monkey bars when children are pulling their body up continue to strengthen the hand in not only supporting strength of grip but also fine motor skills. Swimming is also recognised as a positive activity to support the smaller muscles in the hands.

Muscles in the forearm control the movements in the elbow, wrist and fingers, whilst the smaller movements within the palm of the hand control those of the fingers and thumbs, supporting finger isolation and thumb opposition (movement of the thumb to touch each fingertip on the same hand).

The development of control and strengthening of these muscles is supportive of a good and relaxed pincer grip, providing fluidity when writing. Children's hands will soon become tired

if they have a strong pencil grip. If appropriate to support a child's individual needs then the use of triangular pencils or pencil grips may be helpful.

The working together of the visual and motor systems, using the eyes to guide the hand (eye–hand coordination), enables the child to move around and respond to objects with accuracy (Wilson, 1999). This plays a crucial part in early writing.

Crossing the midline and bilateral coordination

Chapter 2 highlighted the importance of early movement in supporting the transferring of information across the midline. In the context of early writing, the swapping of the pencil from one hand to the other, writing predominately down one side of the page and not being able to hold the paper still to support the writing hand can be indicators that this is difficult for a child. The child may try to position their body at varying angles or move the paper in an attempt to support themselves and complete the activity.

CASE STUDY

Taj

Taj's preferred and dominant hand for writing is his left. Using good pencil control, Taj can be seen to hold his pencil and form letters well. When writing, he starts at the left-hand side of the page and writes across as far as the middle before starting a new line.

Reflective question

» *Whilst 'smiley' faces and stickers may act as an incentive to write across the whole page, how else might you look to support Taj to comfortably write across the whole page?*

Retained primitive reflexes

Chapter 1 identified primitive reflexes and described how movement supports them in being diminished to a healthy level. It is important that the grasp reflex is integrated well so that the pincer grip can develop to support early writing. If this does not happen the child may: (Blomberg, 2011)

- display poor fine motor skills and therefore poor writing;

- have an inappropriate pencil grip causing the pencil to be held too tightly;

- express discomfort in their back and shoulders when seated at a desk.

Activities and resources

In continuing to support motor development and sensory integration the list below offers you a range of indoor and outdoor fine motor activities and resources that through holding, manipulating, reaching, grasping, lifting, pushing and pulling are beneficial to children's early writing. Again, as with any provision you would need to risk-assess them appropriately.

- Offer a range of malleable materials such as dough and clay to support manipulation skills and sensory integration.

- Baking opportunities and mud kitchens further develop wrist rotation through stirring, whisking and mixing, whilst rolling and patting offer fine motor strength.

- Provide washing lines and pegs, buttons, zips and laces and padlocks and keys, all of which give children opportunities to develop fine motor control.

- Sensory activities involving finger paint, cornflour and sand offer great mark-making opportunities alongside developing finger isolation.

- Pincers, pegs, chopsticks, pipettes, squirty bottles and toys all support the development of the pincer grasp.

- Posting, threading and weaving, construction and jigsaws enhance eye–hand coordination and support the use of both hands together.

- Engaging children in action songs, finger puppets, books and stories not only support language development but that of wrist rotation and finger isolation.

- Be creative in role play and mark-making areas of provision, following children's interests.

- Give children time and space to use small elastic bands and Lycra to pull and stretch.

- Offering resources within the sand and water areas for filling, lifting, sieving and pouring all continue to develop fine motor strength and coordination. Sponges are supportive of developing and strengthening children's grasp.

- Ensure a variety of textured objects for young children to reach, grasp and explore.

Senses

An understanding of the senses in relation to early writing is essential.

- **Tactile sense**. Supporting children in their ability to process tactile sensations such as pressure and movement is crucial. We receive tactile information through the receptors in our skin. This sense therefore supports the many tactile sensations involved in writing. 'Reading, writing, and arithmetic ... are extremely complex processes that can develop only upon a strong foundation of sensory integration' (Ayres, 2005, p 11). Children who find it difficult to discriminate between sensations may find it hard to manipulate and use mark-making implements. Time spent on the tummy in the prone position and the opening up of the palm and weight-bearing is supportive here.

- **Proprioception sense.** As identified in Chapters 1 and 2 proprioception sense enables knowing where your body is in space and judging and perceiving distance. In relating this to early writing there is the need not only to effectively navigate the pencil in relation to the paper but also to apply the correct amount of pressure whilst holding a pencil. Without these abilities we witness two familiar outcomes: the child who applies too much pressure every time they go to use the pencil, causing the point to continually break; and the very opposite, the child who holds the pencil so lightly that after being engaged in their writing for a period of time there is only a handful of very faint, light marks on the page. It is therefore important to support children in developing strength in their hands, arms and shoulders (Macintyre and McVitty, 2004). In the long term this sense also supports the ability to engage in the process of looking at a screen and transferring marks to paper. Time spent on the tummy, crawling and creeping are supportive of the development of this sense.

- **Vestibular sense.** The ability to comfortably sit up and remain sitting up, maintaining balance and coordination centrally, is fundamental for children to comfortably sit on a chair at a table. Sitting still is the hardest movement for children to achieve, so supporting this process is fundamental. Time given to engage in linear and rotary movements will support the development of this sense.

CASE STUDY

Homework

The teacher of a combined Reception/Year 1 class shared that during a recent parents' evening a number of parents had commented that their child was finding it difficult to complete their written homework. A variety of suggestions to support the children had been offered, including permitting children to complete their homework on their tummy on the floor. Over the subsequent weeks further conversations with the parents had taken place to identify if there had been any change. The teacher shared that the most consistent and positive response from parents was where children had completed their homework on their tummy. They commented that their child completed their homework quicker, it was 'less of a battle' and their child was more interested in learning.

Reflective question

» *What movement opportunities could you encourage children to experience and participate in that would, over time, support them to complete their homework sitting up?*

Positioning

Equal importance should be given to supporting children in developing good pencil grip and posture to ensure that they are comfortable when writing, therefore guarding against tired and aching muscles and limbs. You should take into consideration the height of the table, so that the child is comfortable and the shoulders are in a relaxed position providing ease in connecting with paper/surface. In supporting children's individual needs you should consider the use of writing slopes/boards to prevent unnecessary stretching and reaching over

the paper. As established in Chapter 2, the need for a child's feet to have contact with the floor ensures strong sensory feedback, enabling a secure sense of where their body is, therefore supporting good levels of concentration.

Knowing and considering a child's preferred/dominant hand will enable children to sit at a table with the right amount of room to engage in their writing. Children who write with their left hand will be best placed at the left-hand side of the table next to a peer who is right-handed, enabling the smooth flow of movement and plenty of room for both children (Foundation Years, 2009).

Left-handed children will often position their paper to the left side of the centre of their body on a slight tilt, enabling them to see what they are writing. Smudging can also be a problem for left-handed children, so encouraging them to hold the pencil a little from the end (1.5–2 cm) can be helpful. Given that left-handed children find it more natural to write from right to left (mirror writing), then marking the starting point at the left hand side of the paper will give them direction.

CASE STUDY

Jake

Jake is 5 years old and his preferred and dominant hand is his right. When asked to sit on the chair at the table to engage in writing activities, he demonstrates a reluctance and discomfort in his body.

After sitting for a few moments trying intently to find an easy way of holding his pencil so that he can communicate his thoughts and ideas, he is observed supporting and holding his right arm.

When asked if everything is OK, he replies 'My arm is tired, it hurts.' With encouragement, Jake would try a little longer before moving around on his chair in an attempt to reposition himself and become comfortable. He would alternate between sitting upright, moving around on his chair and leaning forwards into the table, resting his head on his right arm.

At the end of the activity very little had been accomplished.

Reflective question

» *How would you support Jake in becoming comfortable in his body to enable him to engage in his writing? Explain your ideas.*

Supporting early mark-making within provision

Children make marks from an early age. They do so long before they can hold a pencil and write a word. Opportunities that support the development of gross and fine motor skills needed for early writing should be a part of your daily provision.

Experimentation and exploration

Babies and young children need opportunities and encouragement to experiment with sensory and tactile materials in order to become confident mark makers. The provision of large open spaces, time and freedom to explore natural and recycled resources will help children develop their coordination, motor skills and positive dispositions to mark making. An important benefit to this type of mark making provision is in the fact that the marks made, for example, in the sand, are not permanent, and control for making changes or re-exploring is held by the child.

(Department for Children, Schools and Families, 2008, p 26)

CASE STUDY

Creative play and early marking

As a setting we had received training looking at the importance of early movement and mark-making.

Challenged by the key messages, we reflected on our current creative provision across the whole of our setting.

We identified that creative opportunities were happening predominantly at tables and chairs or at easels and were often adult-led and not open-ended. As a team we agreed that these were limited and not independently accessible to all children.

We explored and discussed how we could enhance the areas, in particular to foster the link between movement and early writing.

We agreed that we would:

- offer large, floor-based creative activities;
- provide open-ended resources that were accessible to the children;
- enhance mark-making opportunities outdoors;
- offer both vertical and horizontal mark-making activities throughout the whole of our provision;
- ensure we were observing and monitoring children's progress;
- effectively share with parents/carers the changes we were making.

As a result:

- boys who had previously shown very little interest in mark-making were suddenly involved and willing to have a go;
- children appeared more comfortable in their bodies whilst engaging in activities;

- children's levels of engagement were higher in the open-ended opportunities;

- language was richer as children shared their ideas and creations;

- parents commented on the increased number of paintings and drawings their children were taking home.

Reflective question

» *The case study highlights that following changes made by the setting there was an increased interest from boys in creative mark-making opportunities. How would you seek to engage boys in early mark-making? Give examples.*

Mark-making area

While mark-making opportunities should indeed be offered throughout early years provision, there should also be a recognised area offering a wide range of resources (Whitehead, 1997) that present children with open-ended experiences to develop the muscles needed to engage in writing. Examples of resources to include are:

- various pens, pencils and mark-making implements;

- a variety of different shapes and sizes of paper, envelopes, card, Post-its, labels;

- diaries, notebooks, calendars, invitations, postcards;

- scissors, tape, pencil sharpener, paper clips, glue sticks;

- fasteners, hole punch, string, pegs;

- clip boards, notice boards;

- laminated cards – letters, numbers and names.

As with any development and enhancement of an area of provision, follow the children's interests that are meaningful to them.

The importance of language

Writing is a form of communication based on thoughts, ideas and creative thinking that is dependent on proficient listening and understanding and the use of spoken language. It is the process of internal thoughts and pictures becoming externally displayed through the use of written marks and symbols.

Children with speech, language and communication needs (SLCN) may also have some difficulties with aspects of reading and writing (I CAN, 2009).

Role play, creating and acting out stories, listening to and reading stories, singing, rhymes and the use of language encouraging movement and space all support children in making marks. Here the connections between the brain, language and motor and sensory development come together (Latham, 2002). You should be mindful of this and make it fundamental to your practice.

The practitioner's role

Children's experiences of mark-making can vary considerably. As a practitioner you can support children in early writing in the following ways:

- Provide movement opportunities to support gross and fine motor development.

- Offer a wide range of sensory activities.

- Ensure that mark-making is available throughout both indoor and outdoor provision (Featherstone and Clarke, 2009).

- Value and display children's mark-making/writing (Bromley, 2006).

- Use a creative and inclusive approach to support language opportunities.

- Present a wide variety of both printed and handwritten text and provide shared writing experiences (Godwin and Perkins, 2002).

- Tune in to children's interests and strengths to support meaningful mark-making.

As with any aspect of learning, creating an emotional environment in which children feel secure, confident, able to take risks and engage in new activities is imperative. Interested practitioners who value and respond positively to children's creative ideas, thoughts and stories are essential in children becoming 'writers'.

Practical tasks

'Writing is a movement skill' (Macintyre, 2007, p 110).

Reflect on a setting that you are currently working in or have recently worked in.

» *Indentify the areas of provision that strongly support gross and fine motor opportunities. Provide examples of each.*

» *Indentify those areas of provision that you recognise need enhancing to further support this. Again, give examples and suggest how they might be improved.*

Reflective questions

» *Within your practice how can you ensure that children learn to write on the basis of their developmental needs rather than what is expected chronologically?*

» *A parent of a 3-year-old child in your setting approaches you and asks 'When is my child going to learn to write?' Firstly, how do you respond whilst supporting them in moving on from the thought that their child is 'just playing'? Secondly, how could you further develop this parental partnership?*

> » *Consider and give examples of how you would develop an inclusive ethos.*

> » *Children who find writing difficult may know the correct answer but display the wrong one. How would you support these children? Explain your answer.*

Summary

The wider the range of possibilities we offer children, the more intense will be their motivations and the richer their experiences.
Loris Malaguzzi (taken from Fraser and Gestwicki, 2002, p 99)

Writing is a means of communication made up of letters, words and symbols that represent language. This chapter has established how motor development and sensory integration are fundamental parts of the process in supporting children in their early writing. Acknowledging that good handwriting is an important part of learning and one that supports children through the education system, it has highlighted that there is a clear need for effective movement spaces and a good range of mark-making resources and opportunities across early years provision that will inspire, challenge and motivate our youngest children.

Further reading

The following website, article and book will continue to provide you with increased knowledge in this area, and importantly will further offer practical ideas that would be helpful for you to incorporate within your everyday practice.

Buckner, M K (n.d.) Hand arches. [online] Available at: www.therapystreetforkids.com/fm-handarches2.html, accessed 30 March 2015.

Clarke, J (2013) Let Them Run and Jump before They Write. *Early Years Update*, 110, July/August 2013, Optimus Education.

Featherstone, S and Clarke, J (2009) *Young Boys and Their Writing: Engaging Young Boys in the Writing Process.* London: A&C Black/Featherstone Education.

References

Ayres, A J (2005) *Sensory Integration and the Child: Understanding Hidden Sensory Challenges*, 25th anniversary edition. Los Angeles: Western Psychological Services.

Blomberg, H (2011) *Movements That Heal: Rhythmic Movement Training and Primitive Reflex Integration.* Sunnybank Hills, QLD, Australia: BookPal.

Bromley, H (2006) *Making My Own Mark: Play and Writing.* London: Early Education: The British Association for Early Childhood Education.

Buckner, M K (n.d.) Hand arches. [online] Available at: www.therapystreetforkids.com/fm-handarches2.html, accessed 30 March 2015.

Bryce Clegg, A (2013) Dough gym week: gross motor physical development. [online] Available at: www.abcdoes.com/abc-does-a-blog/2013/09/dough-gym-week-gross-motor-physical-development/, accessed 30 March 2015.

Clarke, J (2013) Let Them Run and Jump before They Write. *Early Years Update*, 110, July/August 2013, Optimus Education.

Department for Children, Schools and Families (2008) *Mark Making Matters: Young Children Making Meaning in All Areas of Learning and Development*. Nottingham: Department for Children, Schools and Families.

Early Education (2012) *Developmental Matters in the Early Years Foundation Stage (EYFS)*. London: Early Education: The British Association for Early Childhood Education.

Featherstone, S and Clarke, J (2009) *Young Boys and Their Writing: Engaging Young Boys in the Writing Process*. London: A&C Black/Featherstone Education.

Foundation Years (2009) Gateway to writing: developing handwriting. [online] Available at: www.foundationyears.org.uk/2011/10/gateway-to-writing-developing-handwriting/, accessed 30 March 2015.

Fraser, S and Gestwicki, C (2002) *Authentic Childhood: Exploring Reggio Emilia in the Classroom*. Clifton Park, NY: Cengage Learning.

Godwin, D and Perkins, M (2002) *Teaching Language and Literacy in the Early Years*, 2nd edition. London: David Fulton.

Hannaford, C (2005) *Smart Moves: Why Learning Is Not All in Your Head*, 2nd edition. Salt Lake City, UT: Great River Books.

I CAN (2009) *Speech, Language and Communication Needs and Literacy Difficulties*. I CAN Talk Series 1. London: I CAN. Available at: www.ican.org.uk/~/media/Ican2/Whats%20the%20Issue/Evidence/1%20Communication%20Disability%20and%20Literacy%20Difficulties%20pdf.ashx, accessed 30 March 2015.

Latham, D (2002) *How Children Learn to Write: Supporting and Developing Children's Writing in School*. London: Paul Chapman.

Macintyre, C (2007) *Understanding Children's Development in the Early Years: Questions Practitioners Frequently Ask*. Abingdon: Routledge.

Macintyre, C and McVitty, K (2004) *Movement and Learning in the Early Years: Supporting Dyspraxia (DCD) and Other Difficulties*. London: Paul Chapman.

Palmer, S and Corbett, P (2003) *Literacy: What Works? The Golden Rules of Primary Literacy and How You Can Use Them in Your Classroom*. Cheltenham: Nelson Thornes.

Pape, K (2013) Movement starts with the core. [online] Available at: www.karenpapemd.com/index.php/movement-starts-with-the-core/, accessed 30 March 2015.

Whitehead, M R (1997) *Language and Literacy in the Early Years*, 2nd edition. London: Paul Chapman.

Wilson, F R (1999) *The Hand: How Its Use Shapes the Brain, Language, and Human Culture*. New York: Vintage Books.

5 Early movement and supporting boys' learning

Key messages

- It is important to acknowledge the different ways in which boys and girls learn.

- Boys are not less able than girls. Understanding how to effectively engage boys in their learning is critical.

- Being mindful of the links between physical, cognitive and emotional development, it is essential that practitioners know how to recognise the strengths and needs of boys and are able to support these through providing an enabling environment.

- Children do not learn well in stressful situations and environments. They learn more in environments which are secure and offer challenge and with practitioners who know how to positively support their needs. Therefore creating a supportive environment for boys' learning is crucial.

Introduction

All children are unique. In acknowledging that not all children fit the same pattern, this chapter highlights some of the *general* characteristics and differences between boys' and girls' learning within the early years. There are of course many differences within groups of boys, and girls, as well as between them. Whilst being mindful of the links with cognitive and emotional development, the focus remains on physical development.

The question of nature versus nurture has been a topical one for many years within early years practice. Whilst the aim of this chapter is not to debate this, it may offer you a wider perspective.

Recent national EYFSP data results generally indicate that boys are achieving less well in comparison to girls. Therefore, in recognising that there needs to be a change in these outcomes, what needs to be done differently? Equally relevant, are boys underachieving or are they achieving at the level they should be within the early years?

> *Being politically correct has disadvantaged everyone because equal does not mean that everyone is the same. The principle which replaced 'to each according to their need' with 'everyone should have the same', has let everyone down.*
> *The vast majority of parents and education professionals will say this view can no longer be supported. They spend their days working and playing with both boys and girls, and they know that boys and girls are different; that even when you take away race, colour and religion, boys and girls behave differently, are interested in different things and are switched on to learning in different ways.*
>
> (Featherstone and Bayley, 2010, p 5)

The differences in the brain

The brain has two hemispheres, both of which are important in and support aspects of learning (Healy, 2004). (See Table 5.1, which lists some of the general differences between the two hemispheres.)

Table 5.1 The two hemispheres of the brain

Left hemisphere	*Right hemisphere*
Provides detail	Sees whole
Reasons logically	Reasons intuitively
Language: speech, letter sounds and grammar	Language: pitch, gesture, prosody (melody), social interaction
Planned – structured	Spontaneous – fluid
Language-orientated	Feelings-/experience-orientated
Numbers	Images, intuition
Technique	Flow and movement

Source: From Healy, 2004, p 149, Hannaford, 2005, p 90.

At birth the brain contains about 100 billion specialised brain cells called neurons (Dommett, 2012). All babies are born with the same amount of linked cells. Boys have most of their linked cells in separate halves of the brain, with more in the right side (Featherstone and Bailey, 2009). Girls already have some of their linked cells in both halves of the brain. Connections between the two sides of the brain are made through the corpus callosum (the bundle of nerve fibres connecting the left and right hemispheres). The corpus callosum tends to be larger in girls (Gurian, 2010). Whilst the left side of the brain develops more slowly in all babies, this is more pronounced in boys.

The left side of the brain develops more slowly in boys and the necessary links between the hemispheres to facilitate reading often don't develop until boys are between six and eight.

(Featherstone and Bayley, 2010, p 16)

The fact that boys' and girls' brains develop differently gives perspective on why a boy and girl of the same chronological age can be at different development stages (Farmer, 2012).

In terms of language, the majority of girls often talk earlier than boys (Healy, 2004). It is not unusual for girls to use verbal communication to express themselves where boys may choose to use non-verbal communication as their means of expression. What is also helpful to acknowledge is that girls use the language centres in both sides of the brain, while boys' language is often still processed in the right side. This makes it difficult for boys to separate talking and moving (Featherstone and Bayley, 2010).

Testosterone

Hormones also effect learning. Boys have a higher level of testosterone than girls. At around age 4, boys have a sudden surge of testosterone (Fleetham, 2008). This frequently presents itself in active play and lower impulse control. The release of testosterone increases strength, often making boys stronger and more competitive and aggressive than girls. This is frequently evident in physical play and activities.

Differences in learning

Continual observation within an early years environment shows differences in the way boys and girls learn. It is important that you understand and perceive these correctly.

Boys are physical and active learners. The development of fine motor skills often develops later in boys than in girls. Boys tend to take up more room when they are learning and spread their things out over a large space (Gurian, 1996). This is something to bear in mind when considering whether your setting is supportive of the ways boys learn. As impulse control is lower in boys, movement opportunities offer a positive means in which they can engage, especially in more formal classroom activities. Alongside gross motor activities you may want to consider the means of movement used to engage in activities. It is also acknowledged that girls get bored less easily than boys (Gurian, 2010), so there is a need to recognise the need that boys have to move whilst engaging in their learning.

Boys tend to prefer to learn more through activities and movement than they do through sitting and listening. In order to sit still you need to have control over your body. This is the most advanced level of movement and therefore the hardest for children to achieve. Boys often cannot sit still for as long as girls can (Farmer, 2012). (See Table 5.2 for a summary of developmental gender differences.)

Table 5.2 Developmental gender differences and tendencies.

Male (pre-school)	Female (pre-school)
Occupies larger space on the playground than girls	Congregates in groups of other girls in smaller spaces, often huddling together
Playground activities involve more individual running Playground games are rough and vigorous, competitive and aggressive	Playground games are quieter and less active, more cooperative
Playing with blocks, builds high structures likely to topple over	Playing with blocks, tends to build low and long structures
Games involve bodily contact, tumbling, continuous flow of action	Games involve turn taking and indirect competition most of the time
Shorter attention span and less empathy	Greater attention span and empathy

Source: From the book *Boys and Girls Learn Differently* (Gurian, 2010, p 35). The table gives a small selection from the section on developmental gender differences and tendencies, pre-school. There are of course many other differences.

CASE STUDY

The need to move to learn

Akachi was the first to volunteer for any request given by his teacher, which gave him an opportunity to get up and move away from his chair. These activities included giving out books and delivering messages. Given the opportunity, he would prefer to do his writing lying down on the floor and stand up and walk about when reading his book. It was also noticeable that during story time on the carpet, Akachi could also be seen to have something in his hand or pocket to hold and play with. Initially this was thought to be disruptive and unhelpful to his learning; however, closer observation showed that when Akachi was 'moving' his levels of well-being and involvement were significantly higher. As a result, acceptable movement activities were incorporated into the daily routine and provision, which continued to support his learning.

Reflective questions

» *Given that movement stimulates the brain, what opportunities do you give boys to move around during more formal classroom activities? List and share your thoughts, reflecting on how often and for how long you ask boys to sit still.*

» *Is boys' natural desire to move recognised and valued or is it seen and perceived to be disruptive? How might you bring about positive change if this is the case?*

CASE STUDY

A practitioner's response: reflective practice

As a practitioner working in a nursery with Foundation Stage children I would continually seek to observe and reflect on the way the children accessed and engaged within the areas of provision available. With a 70 per cent cohort of boys I would frequently observe them seeking to build tall and creative towers. I would equally see them display and vocalise their frustration when they heard a practitioner say, 'Be careful' or 'Please don't build that too high, it may fall over and hurt someone.' Considering the importance of safety, there was the challenge of locating the areas within the setting that gave those opportunities for building high whilst managing risk.

Reflective question

» *Reflecting on the case study, what are the areas and opportunities within your current setting, or one that you have visited recently, that support or could be developed to support the desire to build high?*

The earliest years are a critically important time and practitioners have a responsibility to create environments in which young children's learning and development can flourish and their gifts and talents can be recognised, nurtured and extended.

(Department for Children, Schools and Families, 2010, p 3)

Reflective question

» *Whilst acknowledging that all areas of learning are important, do you think physical achievements are given the same recognition and value in your setting? Expand on your answer.*

Creating a supportive environment for boys' learning

The environment is a fundamental resource. Addressing the following questions is crucial in your role as a practitioner to enable you to support boys by providing a rich and enabling environment.

- Where does a lot of boys' learning take place?

- How do boys learn?

- What does this learning look like?

- How is this learning supported?

You may find the following suggestions useful.

- Give lots of opportunities, time and space for movement throughout the day, both indoors and out. Remember the importance of supporting the vestibular, proprioception and tactile senses.

- Ensure learning takes place outdoors.

- Ensure that you give lots of brain breaks.

- Provide lots of fine motor activities.

- Give lots of 'hands-on' opportunities and provide open-ended resources that can be transported.

- Talk to boys about how to resolve situations without hurting one another.

- Give opportunities for rough-and-tumble play.

- Enable boys to take healthy risks.

Brain breaks

Boys need more down-time for their brains than girls do (Fleetham, 2008). This is referred to as the 'rest state'. Recognised often as 'a gaze', this happens more frequently during the day for boys than it does for girls. The need for brain breaks not only needs to be considered in relation to the opportunities and structure of the day, but also in terms of ensuring that the requests you make of children are realistic.

> *A boy's brain 'shuts off' (enters a rest state) more times a day than a girl's brain tends to do – as a result boys and girls have different approaches to paying attention, visioning their future, completing a task, de-stressing, feeling emotions, relating to others, becoming bored, and even having basic conversations.*
>
> (Gurian, 2009, p 31)

Rough-and-tumble play

Continual observation within the early years highlights that boys are generally more physical. It is not unusual for boys to seek opportunities for physical contact through rough-and-tumble play. Providing positive opportunities for rough-and-tumble play and supporting them is important.

> *[R]ough and tumble play, such as wrestling, in the early years can provide boys with tactile experiences and help them to develop physical fitness and sensory awareness and also help to regulate their strength and self control.*
>
> (Rawstrone, 2011, p 24)

Stress

> *Playtime should be relaxed and pressure-free.*
> (Healy, 2004, p 68)

Children do not learn well in stressful situations and environments. Stress causes anxious behaviour, making it more difficult to think and making learning difficult.

> *[T]he emotional brain [can] overpower, even paralyze the thinking brain. Students who are anxious, angry, or depressed don't learn; people who are caught in these states do not take in information effectively or deal with it well.*
>
> (Goleman, 1996, p 78)

Children should learn in an environment which is developmentally appropriate, provides challenge and in which they are secure. This should be with practitioners who know how to respond to and meet their needs. Reflect on this in relation to your setting or one that you have visited recently. Share your thoughts in response.

It may also be helpful here to be mindful of Maslow's hierarchy of needs (Wilson, 2008). It is a clear reminder of the basic human needs that have to be met for all children, without which there is a significant impact on learning.

The practitioner's role

Alongside providing the right environment for children to engage and learn, the response of the practitioner is of paramount importance. Knowledgeable practitioners who observe, listen, positively interact and sensitively support will provide a difference to children within the early years.

The list below offers you ways in which you can support boys in your setting:

- know and build on their interests;
- find meaningful ways to engage them in their learning;
- acknowledge that they are active learners;
- value their physicality/movement;
- support their strengths;
- know their learning preferences;
- support their creativity;
- provide lots of opportunities for problem solving;
- talk about, display and value their contributions;
- celebrate what they can do and build up their self-esteem.

It is crucial that as a team you address gender issues and make sure that positive images and resources are a part of your provision.

Practical tasks

» *Identify and develop a range of positive gender images and resources that you would want to have within your setting.*

» *Within an early years setting, observe the differences between boys and girls. Using your observations and focusing on one of the differences you have observed relating to physical development, plan how you are going to respond in order to support boys in their learning.*

Reflective questions

» *How have you positively sought to channel boys' energy?*

» *How have you recently used the interests of boys to support their learning? Give an example.*

» *How are boys supported in your setting? Is there a consistent approach within the team? Is there more you can do to enhance and develop this approach?*

» *What are some of the familiar assumptions made about boys? List them and explain why these are not helpful.*

» *Reflecting on impulsive behaviour, how can you support boys to think before acting?*

» *Boys will often engage in superhero play. How do you positively support this? What learning is taking place?*

» *Given the different ways boys and girls learn; share your thoughts on the current assessment frameworks. Are they equally supportive of both boys and girls?*

Summary

> *Since we cannot change reality, let us change the eyes which see reality.*
> Kazantzakis (n.d.)

This chapter has focused on identifying some of the ways that boys and girls learn differently. It has sought to explain this through an examination of brain development and has offered suggestions for how to engage boys in an enabling environment.

> *Creating the right conditions for children to develop confidence in themselves as learners, explorers, discoverers and critical thinkers is vital in a rapidly changing world. This is particularly important for boys as their natural exuberance, energy and keen exploratory drive may often be misinterpreted. Unwittingly, boys can be labelled and their behaviour perceived as inappropriate or even challenging. The qualities and skills that are most valued by schools, the ability to communicate orally and represent ideas on paper, are often the very aspects of learning that boys find the most difficult.*
> (Department for Children, Schools and Families, 2007, p 3)

Further reading

The following books will provide you with a more detailed picture of the differences in boys' and girls' brains and their impact on learning.

Fleetham, M (2008) *How To ... Understand and Improve Boys' Learning.* Nottingham: LDA.

Gurian, M (2010) *Boys and Girls Learn Differently: A Guide for Teachers and Parents*, 10th anniversary edition. San Francisco: Jossey-Bass.

References

Department for Children, Schools and Families (2007) *Primary National Strategy. Confident, Capable and Creative: Supporting Boys' Achievements: Guidance for Practitioners in the Early Years Foundation Stage.* Nottingham: Department for Children, Schools and Families.

Department for Children, Schools and Families (2010) *National Strategies Early Years. Finding and Exploring Young Children's Fascinations: Strengthening the Quality of Gifted and Talented Provision in the Early Years.* Nottingham: Department for Children, Schools and Families.

Dommett, E (2012) The Structure of the Human Brain, in Woodhead M and Oates, J (eds) *Early Childhood in Focus 7: Developing Brains.* Milton Keynes: Open University.

Farmer, N (2012) *Getting It Right for Boys: Why Boys Do What They Do and How to Make the Early Years Work for Them.* London: Bloomsbury/Featherstone Education.

Featherstone, S and Bayley, R (2009) *Boys and Girls Come Out to Play: Not Better or Worse, Just Different.* London: A&C Black/Featherstone Education.

Featherstone, S and Bayley, R (2010) *The Cleverness of Boys: Understanding What Boys Do Well and Helping Them to Succeed.* London: A&C Black/Featherstone Education.

Fleetham, M (2008) *How To ... Understand and Improve Boys' Learning.* Nottingham: LDA.

Goleman, D (1996) *Emotional Intelligence: Why It Can Matter More Than IQ.* New York: Bantam Books.

Gurian, M (1996) *The Wonder of Boys: What Parents, Mentors and Educators Can Do to Shape Boys into Exceptional Men.* New York: Tarcher/Putnam Books.

Gurian, M (2009) *The Purpose of Boys: Helping Our Sons Find Meaning, Significance and Direction in Their Lives.* San Francisco: Jossey-Bass.

Gurian, M (2010) *Boys and Girls Learn Differently: A Guide for Teachers and Parents*, 10th anniversary edition. San Francisco: Jossey-Bass.

Hannaford, C (2005) *Smart Moves: Why Learning Is Not All in Your Head*, 2nd edition. Salt Lake City, UT: Great River Books.

Healy, J M (2004) *Your Child's Growing Mind: Brain Development and Learning from Birth to Adolescence*, 3rd edition. New York: Broadway Books.

Kazantzakis, N (n.d.) Brainy Quotes. [online] Available at: www.brainyquote.com/quotes/authors/n/nikos_kazantzakis.html, accessed 30 March 2015.

Rawstrone, A (2011) A Unique Child: Wrestling – Roll with It. *Nursery World*, 6 January 2011.

Wilson, G (2008) *Help Your Boys Succeed: The Essential Guide for Parents.* London: Continuum.

References

Angelou, M (n.d.) Brainy Quotes. [online] Available at: www.brainyquote.com/quotes/authors/m/maya_angelou.html, accessed 4 April 2015.

Atherton, F and Nutbrown, C (2013) *Understanding Schemas and Young Children: From Birth to Three.* London: Sage.

Ayres, A J (2005) *Sensory Integration and the Child: Understanding Hidden Sensory Challenges*, 25th anniversary edition. Los Angeles: Western Psychological Services.

Bilton, H (2014) *Playing Outside: Activities, Ideas and Inspiration for the early years*, 2nd edition. Abingdon: Routledge.

Blomberg, H (2011) *Movements That Heal: Rhythmic Movement Training and Primitive Reflex Integration.* Sunnybank Hills, QLD, Australia: BookPal.

Bly, L (2011) *Components of Typical and Atypical Motor Development.* Laguna Beach, CA Neuro-Development Treatment Association, Inc.

Brodie, K (2013) *Observation, Assessment and Planning in the Early Years: Bringing It All Together.* Maidenhead, Berkshire: Open University Press.

Bromley, H (2006) *Making My Own Mark: Play and Writing.* London: Early Education: The British Association for Early Childhood Education.

Bruce, T (2004) *Developing Learning in Early Childhood: 0–8 years.* London: Sage.

Bruce, T (2005) *Early Childhood Education*, 3rd edition. London: Hodder Education.

Bryce Clegg, A (2013) Dough gym week: gross motor physical development. [online] Available at: www.abcdoes.com/abc-does-a-blog/2013/09/dough-gym-week-gross-motor-physical-development/, accessed 30 March 2015.

Buckner, M K (n.d.) Hand arches. [online] Available at: www.therapystreetforkids.com/fm-handarches2.html, accessed 30 March 2015.

Chilvers, D (2006) *Young Children Talking: The Art of Conversation and Why Children Need to Chatter.* London: Early Education: The British Association for Early Childhood Education.

Clarke, J (2013) Let Them Run and Jump before They Write. *Early Years Update*, 110, July/August 2013, Optimus Education.

Clarke, J (2014) Physical Activities to Underpin PSED. *Early Years*, June 2014, Optimus Education.

Department for Children, Schools and Families (2007) *Primary National Strategy. Confident, Capable and Creative: Supporting Boys' Achievements: Guidance for Practitioners in the Early Years Foundation Stage.* Nottingham: Department for Children, Schools and Families.

Department for Children, Schools and Families (2008) *Mark Making Matters: Young Children Making Meaning in All Areas of Learning and Development.* Nottingham: Department for Children, Schools and Families.

Department for Children, Schools and Families (2010) *National Strategies Early Years. Finding and Exploring Young Children's Fascinations: Strengthening the Quality of Gifted and Talented Provision in the Early Years.* Nottingham: Department for Children, Schools and Families.

Department for Education (2012) *Statutory Framework for the Early Years Foundation Stage: Setting the Standards for Learning, Development and Care for Children from Birth to Five.* Runcorn, Cheshire: Department for Education.

Dommett, E (2012) The Structure of the Human Brain, in Woodhead M and Oates, J (eds) *Early Childhood in Focus 7: Developing Brains.* Milton Keynes: Open University.

Early Education (2012) *Developmental Matters in the Early Years Foundation Stage (EYFS).* London: Early Education: The British Association for Early Childhood Education.

Farmer, N (2012) *Getting It Right for Boys: Why Boys Do What They Do and How to Make the Early Years Work for Them.* London: Bloomsbury/Featherstone Education.

Featherstone, S (2008) Practice Makes Perfect: How the Growing Brain Makes Sense of Experiences, in Featherstone, Sand Featherstone, P, *Like Bees, Not Butterflies: Child-Initiated Learning in the Early Years.* London: A&C Black/Featherstone Education.

Featherstone, S and Bayley, R (2009) *Boys and Girls Come Out to Play: Not Better or Worse, Just Different.* London: A&C Black/Featherstone Education.

Featherstone, S and Bayley, R (2010) *The Cleverness of Boys: Understanding What Boys Do Well and Helping Them to Succeed.* London: A&C Black/Featherstone Education.

Featherstone, S and Clarke, J (2009) *Young Boys and Their Writing: Engaging Young Boys in the Writing Process.* London: A&C Black/Featherstone Education.

Featherstone, S and Louis, S (2013) *Understanding Schemas in Young Children: Again! Again!*, 2nd edition. London: Bloomsbury/Featherstone Education.

Fleetham, M (2008) *How To ... Understand and Improve Boys' Learning.* Nottingham: LDA.

Foundation Years (2009) Gateway to writing: developing handwriting. [online] Available at: www.foundationyears.org.uk/2011/10/gateway-to-writing-developing-handwriting/, accessed 30 March 2015.

Fraser, S and Gestwicki, C (2002) *Authentic Childhood: Exploring Reggio Emilia in the Classroom.* Clifton Park, NY: Cengage Learning.

Goddard Blythe, S (2005) *The Well Balanced Child: Movement and Early Learning*, revised edition. Stroud, Gloucestershire: Hawthorn Press.

Goddard Blythe, S (2008) *What Babies and Children Really Need.* Stroud, Gloucestershire: Hawthorn Press.

Godwin, Dand Perkins, M (2002) *Teaching Language and Literacy in the Early Years*, 2nd edition. London: David Fulton.

Goleman, D (1996) *Emotional Intelligence: Why It Can Matter More Than IQ.* New York: Bantam Books.

Greenland, P (2000) *Hopping Home Backwards: Body Intelligence and Movement Play.* Leeds: JABADAO Centre for Movement Studies.

Gurian, M (1996) *The Wonder of Boys: What Parents, Mentors and Educators Can Do to Shape Boys into Exceptional Men.* New York: Tarcher/Putnam Books.

Gurian, M (2009) *The Purpose of Boys: Helping Our Sons Find Meaning, Significance and Direction in Their Lives.* San Francisco: Jossey-Bass.

Gurian, M (2010) *Boys and Girls Learn Differently: A Guide for Teachers and Parents*, 10th anniversary edition. San Francisco: Jossey-Bass.

Hannaford, C (2005) *Smart Moves: Why Learning Is Not All in Your Head*, 2nd edition. Salt Lake City, UT: Great River Books.

Healy, J M (2004) *Your Child's Growing Mind: Brain Development and Learning from Birth to Adolescence*, 3rd edition. New York: Broadway Books.

I CAN (2009) *Speech, Language and Communication Needs and Literacy Difficulties.* I CAN Talk Series 1. London: I CAN. Available at: www.ican.org.uk/~/media/Ican2/Whats%20the%20Issue/Evidence/1%20Communication%20Disability%20and%20Literacy%20Difficulties%20pdf.ashx, accessed 30 March 2015.

JABADAO (2012) Continence issues. [online] Available at: www.jabadao.org, accessed 30 March 2015.

Kamen, T (2013) *Observation and Assessment for the EYFS.* London: Hodder Education.

Kazantzakis, N (n.d.) Brainy Quotes. [online] Available at: www.brainyquote.com/quotes/authors/n/nikos_kazantzakis.html, accessed 30 March 2015.

Laevers, F and Heylen, L (2004) *Involvement of Children and Teacher Style: Insights from an International Study on Experiential Education.* Leuven, Belgium: Leuven University Press. [In addition you may also find the following link helpful: www.earlylearninghq.org.uk/earlylearninghq-blog/the-leuven-well-being-and-involvement-scales/, accessed 30 March 2015.]

Lamont, B (n.d.) The belly crawl. [online] Available at: www.developmentalmovement.org/upload/The%20Belly%20Crawl.pdf, accessed 30 March 2015.

Lamont, B (n.d.) Learning and movement. [online] Available at: www.developmentalmovement.org/upload/Learning%20and%20Movement.pdf, accessed 4 April 2015.

Lane, S J (2002) Structure and Function of the Sensory Systems, in Bundy, A C, Lane, S J and Murray, E A, *Sensory Integration: Theory and Practice*, 2nd edition. Philadelphia: F A Davis Company.

Latham, D (2002) *How Children Learn to Write: Supporting and Developing Children's Writing in School.* London: Paul Chapman.

Maayan, I. (2013) The Embryo Project Encyclopedia: In the womb (2005), by Toby McDonald and National Geographic Channel. [online] Available at: http://embryo.asu.edu/pages/national-geographic-channels-womb, accessed 4 April 2015.

Macintyre, C (2007) *Understanding Children's Development in the Early Years: Questions Practitioners Frequently Ask.* Abingdon: Routledge.

Macintyre, C and McVitty, K (2004) *Movement and Learning in the Early Years: Supporting Dyspraxia (DCD) and Other Difficulties.* London: Paul Chapman.

Montessori, M (n.d.) Daily Montessori. [online] Available at: www.dailymontessori.com/maria-montessori-quotes/, accessed 30 March 2015.

O'Connor, A (2012) A Clean Sweep. *Nursery World, Supplement: Physical Development Special*, May 2012.

O'Connor, A (2014) First Moves. *Nursery World*, 3–16 November 2014.

Palmer, S and Corbett, P (2003) *Literacy: What Works? The Golden Rules of Primary Literacy and How You Can Use Them in Your Classroom.* Cheltenham: Nelson Thornes.

Pape, K (2013) Movement starts with the core. [online] Available at: www.karenpapemd.com/index.php/movement-starts-with-the-core/, accessed 30 March 2015.

Rawstrone, A (2011) A Unique Child: Wrestling– Roll with It. *Nursery World*, 6 January 2011.

Restak, R M (1984) *The Brain.* New York: Bantam.

Roberts, R (2010) *Wellbeing from Birth.* London: Sage.

Samuel, L (n.d.) The brain stem. [online] Available at: www.interactive-biology.com/1835/the-3-parts-of-the-brain-stem-and-their-functions-episode-27/, accessed 4 April 2015.

Stiles, J (2012) Neural Growth and Pruning, in Woodhead, M and Oates, J (eds) *Early Childhood in Focus 7: Developing Brains.* Milton Keynes: Open University.

Stock Kranowitz, C (2003) *The Out-of-Sync Child Has Fun: Activities for Kids with Sensory Processing Disorder*, revised edition. New York: Perigee.

Stock Kranowitz, C (2005) *The Out-of-Sync Child: Recognizing and Coping with Sensory Processing Disorder*, revised edition. New York: Perigee.

Tallack, P (2006) *In the Womb: Witness the Journey from Conception to Birth through Astonishing 3D Images.* Washington, DC: National Geographic.

Tovey, H (2011) Achieving the Balance: Challenge, Risk and Safety, in White, J (ed.) *Outdoor Provision in the Early Years.* London: Sage.

Vine, P (2011) *A Journey from Within.* Leeds: Leeds City Council.

Warden, C (2012) *Nurture through Nature*, 2nd edition. Crieff, Perthshire: Mindstretchers.

White, J (2012) Natural play: It's spring now – why not think about going barefoot! [online] Available at: www.janwhitenaturalplay.wordpress.com/2012/04/09, accessed 30 March 2015.

Whitehead, M R (1997) *Language and Literacy in the Early Years*, 2nd edition. London: Paul Chapman.

Wilson, F R (1999) *The Hand: How Its Use Shapes the Brain, Language, and Human Culture.* New York: Vintage Books.

Wilson, G (2008) *Help Your Boys Succeed: The Essential Guide for Parents.* London: Continuum.

Index